THE MARRIED MAN

BY C. C. Carlson

The Late Great Planet Earth (with Hal Lindsey)

Satan Is Alive and Well on Planet Earth (with Hal Lindsey)

Straw Houses in the Wind

In My Father's House (with Corrie ten Boom)

The Terminal Generation (with Hal Lindsey)

Established in Eden

Woman (with Dale Evans Rogers)

The Married Man (with Bob Vernon)

THE
MARRIED
MAN

Bob Vernon
and C. C. Carlson

FLEMING H. REVELL COMPANY
Old Tappan, New Jersey

Library of Congress Cataloging in Publication Data
Vernon, Bob.
    The married man.
    1. Men—Psychology.   2. Husbands.   3. Fathers.
I. Carlson, Carole C., joint author.   II. Title.
HQ1090.V47   155.6′452   80-12592
ISBN 0-8007-1117-3

Contents

THE MARRIED MAN

1

What role does the married man play? Is he the lovable, authoritarian lead character in *Life With Father*? Is he the prejudiced, bungling Archie Bunker? Is he Caspar Milquetoast or Superman? What makes him restless or satisfied, happy or frustrated?

Here I am, a woman working with a man, to write a book about his role! Questions whirred through my mind about this project. Would the principles of *The Married Man* stand the scrutiny of day-in, day-out pressures? If a man is going to describe the true masculine role, he knows he will be under a magnifying glass; he is vulnerable.

The critics wait in the wings to find the wedge to shake his credibility. No one faces the firing line of public and personal examination more than the person who bares his beliefs before the cynical populace.

To find out about this man, Bob Vernon, I invaded a world that was alien to my background and life-style. Pen and notebook in hand, there I was, right in the middle of the Hollywood Police Station. I looked around and was glad I was just visiting.

I asked to see Commander Mark Kroeker and was escorted through two sets of locked doors before I reached his inner office. It was a bare room. The only thing impressive about it was the man who swung around from behind the desk to shake my hand. Commander Kroeker had been adjutant to Chief Bob Vernon for more than two years. I concluded that he would be a good man to interview.

"I saw more of Bob Vernon on a day-to-day basis than his wife did," he told me. "I listened to his phone conversations, watched him in the daily tensions of police work, and saw him under incredible pressure."

Commander Kroeker told me more about this man who helped shape his life and attitude. "A cop submits to authority," he said, his penetrating eyes narrowed in thought. I wondered if policemen had eyes like that from squinting up gun barrels, but I decided not to ask. "I've never known Bob Vernon to subvert the line of authority, even when he didn't agree with a directive that was given.

"Some people seem to take pride in being free spirits. However, a free spirit is undisciplined and uncoachable. Bob Vernon is a Christian, and a Christian has a submitted spirit.

"The Baretta syndrome seems to be instilled in the public thinking about the police," Kroeker explained. He was referring to a popular television character who solves crimes independently, usually leaving the bumbling police force with egg on their collective faces. Baretta's style ignores authority

"Vernon is not Baretta. He is a coachable guy. He's willing to let his talents be developed by other people."

Commander Kroeker told me Vernon's motto: "Principle versus expediency." Decisions were made upon that concept. If there was a doubt about a course of direction, Vernon would say, "Let's talk about it. What's the principle involved here?"

Principles are ageless, but opinions are personal. I began to realize that this would be a challenge, learning more about *The Married Man.*

After all, every woman *should* know!

C. C.

Masculine Is More Than Macho

What is masculinity? Is it personified by the Friday-night swinger or the Sunday-morning saint? Is this trait distinguished by a haircut or tweed coat? Is this type of man the fellow who exercises his muscles or his brain—or both? *Masculine* has a blurred meaning today. We can buy books on how to dress successfully, we can go to school to improve our minds, we can tan and tone our bodies, but where do we find the source of the true masculine role?

What are the basic character traits that separate the man from the mouse, the leader from the marshmallow?

I have never been able to find an outline for masculine traits in a men's magazine or a job prospectus. Even the dictionary doesn't help. It says that *masculine* means "strong, vigorous, courageous, bold, resolute." *Resolute?* It means "not easily influenced." That lets most of us out. We are all swayed by what others are doing.

However, in evaluating leaders whose masculinity I respected—men whom I have been impelled to follow—I've noticed several consistent qualities in them. First, they are men of integrity.

A Man of Integrity

A man who keeps his word and can be trusted is a man of integrity. In my work, when a man promises he will have four squads of men there within thirty minutes, if I can just hold on with the ten men I have, I know he is the type of man who will deliver. Lives are depending upon him.

A man of integrity keeps and honors his promise to his wife to "forsake all others." He is committed to her.

Too many times the image of the real man is the "man of the world," the one who has more conquests than Don Juan. However, when marriage fidelity is taken lightly, no one wins. King Solomon said, thousands of years ago, *"Above all else, guard your affections. For they influence everything else in your life"* (Proverbs 4:23).

A guy who is loose in his morals and cheats on his wife will have every other aspect of his life influenced. I can spot the fellow in my organization who is messing around with his affections. All he can think about is the next gal he can make. It affects the way he works and the attitudes he has toward his job.

Someone who is really masculine is pure; he does not commit adultery. He is an honest man who doesn't steal the affections of the woman who is not his wife.

If a man is placed in a position of leadership by his church, company, or any other organization, and begins to center his attention on the woman who "understands him better than his wife," his personal leadership ability will begin to dissipate. Remember Delilah? In my opinion, the culprit in that familiar story was not the woman, but Samson, who ignored God's warning concerning the source of his strength and therefore relinquished his leadership as a man of responsibility and character. Delilah was the temptation, but Samson had the choice.

A man of integrity keeps his commitments to his wife, his children, his boss, and his friends.

A Man of Peace

To be masculine, a man should be peaceable. In Proverbs 3:30 it says, "Don't get into needless fights." (It doesn't say not to fight under any circumstances.) Probably the most famous fight of all times was not held in a boxing ring or on a battlefield, but in a temple. Jesus walked into this area, which was supposed to be sacred, and found it swarming with money changers, its places of worship surrounded by the great Jerusalem carnival attractions. He turned over the booths, knocking over the cash registers and scattering the contents of the tables over the cobblestones. This was not a needless fight, but a display of positive strength in confrontation with a specific evil.

When I see some pictures showing Jesus with feminine characteristics, I think that some of the painters must have used women as models. Jesus was the personification of masculinity. He was a carpenter's son, and the men in the building trades of that time couldn't go down to the Jerusalem Lumber Company and order twenty-five two-by-fours. They had to go out into the woods and chop a few trees and hew them by hand. They didn't have band saws. You could tell a carpenter, because he was a "big moose", he was the guy who swung the ax and pulled a mean saw. He didn't have to work out with weights in the gym, after work. He did it every day.

Visualize Jesus striding into the temple and saying, "All right, you guys—move!" They moved! He was a masculine guy with His strength under control. He didn't lose His head. When He was in the Garden of Gethsemane, Judas led a mob of angry men, brandishing swords and clubs, and surrounded Jesus with the brute force that inflamed tempers can bring. Jesus answered their shouts and accusations, and they were so astounded by His strength that they fell back! Even His friends beat it out the back door.

They could have stoned Him to death right then, but they didn't tangle with the carpenter's son. I think we have a mistaken viewpoint of what is masculine and what is godly. We somehow think that the two aren't compatible, but the Bible teaches otherwise. To really be performing God's role as a man is to be a masculine individual, with strength under control. This has nothing to do with size, although I have emphasized the physical strength of Jesus. Obviously, no one has complete control over his size. I'm talking about being the type of man who doesn't mind taking charge and doing what is right. This isn't the fellow who fades into the woodwork when the going gets rough. Proverbs 12:16 says, "A fool is quick-tempered; a wise man stays cool when insulted."

The masculine leader fights when it is necessary to stand up for what is right, but when someone offends him, he stays calm, yet, he does not back down when he is standing for a principle.

I really admire the guy who keeps his head, even though he has a lot of strength. I remember one of the most effective cops I worked with was a guy about six foot five. We walked the beat on Main Street, Los Angeles, back in 1955, when it was really tough. It had all the joints. At the corner of Third and Main, we got into a fight almost every day. This was a hangout for neighborhood warriors, and every time we came down the street they were ready to challenge us. We had to prove that we could lick them. My partner, Gary, was so cool that sometimes the gang members mistook his attitude for one of fear, in spite of his size. They would keep pressing him, taking a swing at him, to test his reactions. When it was necessary to defend himself, watch out! Even I got a little too close when he was winding up to hit someone and took a hard left on my jaw. However, Gary had his strength under control; he never went overboard.

I've seen some policemen lose their heads. Jack Webb put it very well in one of his "Dragnet" shows. He was playing the role of an internal affairs' investigator, who is the man who examines complaints against policemen. A cop was involved in some burglaries. His partner said to him, "Joe, I can't understand it. Look at this guy. He's a Los Angeles police officer . . . caught stealing!"

Joe answered, "Our problem is that we have to recruit from the human race."

Policemen are people, and sometimes, when they begin using force, they go overboard. The adrenalin gets pumping, and they do more thumping than they should. We have to discipline officers when they do that. But Gary wasn't that type. He did what was necessary and then stopped.

A man may not have a lot of physical strength, but may have a strong personality. Some of the strongest men I've known have been small men. They had firm convictions. They were resolute. Have you ever seen pictures of the great men of history? Many of them weren't big men—some of them were pretty puny—but they were strong men.

A Reasonable Man

Another trait of the truly masculine man is that he is reasonable. Proverbs 12:15 says, "A fool thinks he needs no advice, but a wise man listens to others."

I've talked to so many kids who say, "If only my dad would listen to me." I think we have lost the art of communication. Most of us are listening just enough to get the gist of a situation, but we're already thinking of a comeback. Have you ever talked to a person like that? You may have been in a social group and were introduced to someone, started to talk to him, but could see in his eyes that he wasn't hearing a word you were saying. He was thinking of himself and not listening to you at all.

Young people have the ability, more than those of us who are older, to look behind the eyeballs. They see beyond the facade. Our best witnesses in police incidents are young people between the ages of fifteen and twenty-three. They see more, remember more, and are more accurate in their observations.

A reasonable man gets the facts before making a decision. Proverbs 18:13 says, "What a shame—yes, how stupid!—to decide before knowing the facts!"

One of the things that can alienate young people and wives, too, is to know that you don't want any facts. Your mind is made up without listening to what they are saying.

As I have counseled with parents and their children I hear this word *fair* coming up practically every time we have a problem. When I'm trying to be an arbitrator in situations like this, I remember scores of times hearing a young person say, "Yeah, but Dad, that's not fair."

The Bible says that a reasonable, godly man is fair. Proverbs 16:12 says, "It is a horrible thing for a king [or ruler] to do evil. . . ." His right to rule depends on his fairness, his reasonableness.

A Man of Mercy

The man who is assuming his true masculine role is merciful; he responds to the needs of others. "He who shuts his ears to the cries of the poor will be ignored in his own time of need" (Proverbs 21:13). He looks out for the needs of others, especially his own family. He looks out for their psychological needs, for their need to be accepted.

One of the reasons many young people today are doing such bizarre things is because, "I was out with my buddies, and they were doing it."

My usual response is, "Don't you make up your own mind? Why do you do what your buddies do?" They fumble around, but I understand what they are saying. Their peer-group pressure is a very strong motivating force. I've seen it motivate kids to commit murder.

One of the worst stabbing cases I ever handled took place in an urban housing project. I found a kid who had been stabbed in the chest twenty-seven times. By three o'clock that morning, we had rounded up five boys who were involved in this murder, and they were all under the age of seventeen. This was a brutal murder. As I talked to them in separate interrogation rooms, I got the story from each boy and finished with the logical question, "Okay, now. Why?" I asked each of them that question, individually. They all came up with the same story.

One of the boys, Freddie, was mad at another kid for taking out his girl. The gang taunted Freddie by saying, "Hey, here comes the guy who took your girl out." Freddie took the other kid on, knocked him down, and stabbed him. Then he turned and handed the knife to one of the other members of the gang and said, "Come on, you stab him, too. You're one of us." The boy who was telling me the details said, "And when he handed me the knife, I had nothing against the guy. He didn't do anything to me, but I looked around, and all the rest of the guys were looking at me."

I said, "Big deal, they looked at you."

"Yeah, I knew what they were saying with their eyes. 'If you don't do it, you're not part of the group.' So I stabbed him about three times. I didn't want to, but I knew they wanted me to." It seemed so logical to him. "Then I passed it to one of the other guys, and we all looked at him, and he stabbed him a few times."

What motivated these kids to perform such a brutal murder? peer-group pressure. The victim was dying, and, one by one, those boys repeatedly stabbed him, because they wanted so desperately to belong to the group. Some of us can't understand this type of mentality, but the psychologists tell us that the need for acceptance, the need to be loved, is a powerful motivating force.

Many young people don't feel that type of acceptance from their parents. They do feel that from their peer group, and they realize that they can't afford to lose that acceptance.

When I went to Nightingale Junior High, I was a minority student in that school. Marijuana was part of the culture, but I didn't use it. I've often asked myself why that was so. I was an average guy, no different from the rest of the kids. But I remember the factor that made me say no. I'd say, "My dad would die if he found out I smoked marijuana."

My dad was more important to me than my peers. If it were up for grabs whether I would lose my father's acceptance or the acceptance of my buddies, the scale tipped for Dad. He was a real pal to me.

The reason we have more kids falling prey to peer-group pressure today is because we have less of that type of family relationship. We have a different life-style, where everyone is going his own way. We're so interested in making money and doing our thing that we don't spend the time we should together as parents and children.

Many young people today doubt that they are accepted by their dads. They may feel loved, but have some doubt because of Dad's time commitment to them. They'll say, "Well, he tells me he loves me, and I know he does, but. . . ." The *but* usually means, "We don't spend much time together; we don't know each other that well; we don't share that much of our gut-level feelings with each other."

A good husband and father is vitally interested in the needs and concerns of his family members. He is blessed as a man of mercy. In other words, he is a happy man, if he is interested in the needs of others.

A Resolute Man

At the very heart of a man's character are his absolutes, which are more "you" than the clothes you wear or the job you hold.

Why do so many people waver on their position on an issue? Often it's because they haven't taken the time to think through all the implications involved or researched time-tested principles on the subject. In order to be resolute, you have to do your homework.

A man who lives in God's way is unwavering; he has good judgment. *"Learn to be wise,"* he said, *"and develop good judgment and common sense!"* (Proverbs 4:5). This means, men, we must make decisions. I have heard many wives talk about problems in their homes and say, "If only my husband would make a decision. He just won't take a stand. With the kids, for instance, he just lets them make up their own minds. What kind of guidance is that?"

The Bible says we should be resolute and not afraid to exercise bold reproof. "Winking at sin leads to sorrow; bold reproof leads to peace" (Proverbs 10:10).

A Sincere Man

Another trait of masculinity is sincerity. The Bible says "without hypocrisy." *Hypocrisy* has an interesting meaning; it comes from the Greek word that refers to the masks the players wore on stage. The man who is truly masculine is not wearing a mask. He has the guts to reveal his feelings.

Many men are afraid to disclose their true selves, even to their families. They are fearful of showing their weaknesses. When we consider discipline, we're going to see that if we have been wrong, it is important to admit that to our children and our wives. This doesn't detract from leadership capabilities or manliness. It proves the strength of a man when he can say, "Hey, I goofed." He is a person who is so secure that he is able to admit his failings.

None of these character traits of masculinity come naturally. They are the results of time, research, and knowing the facts. Where do we find the source of information about the masculine role? Would you believe that all of the attributes of the masculine leaders are given in one verse in the Bible?

"But the wisdom from above is first pure, then peaceable, gentle, reasonable, full of mercy and good fruits, unwavering, without hypocrisy" (James 3:17 NAS).

That's a real man.

2

Scarlett O'Hara was bold enough to dispel the image of the helpless woman. The Victorian Age put a finis to the delicate female, fainting gracefully midst her satin and ribbons. From the American pioneer wife, to the tailored, modern office worker, women have come a long way.

In spite of our stand for independence, I believe most women like to be around a take-charge man. Many men are not natural leaders; they may have been programmed into vacillation by upbringing or training. When they get married, they are told to be the heads of their families, and they don't have the slightest idea how to function.

One small incident, so insignificant in importance, gave me a clue to a man who was going to draw upon that motto Commander Kroeker gave me: "Principle versus expediency."

I met Bob Vernon for lunch at the Los Angeles Police Academy. As I turned off the freeway, a short distance from metropolitan Los Angeles, I drove up a winding driveway and parked in front of a patio area that was a glimpse into the California Hispanic heritage. A courtyard with cobblestones and fountains, a group of soft pink buildings with tile roofs, the architecture of the classic hacienda provided an unexpected charm. A generous benefactor had gifted the city of Los Angeles with this romantic setting for the rugged training of her police officers. The training given these men is of the same caliber as the rigor and discipline of West Point or the Air Force Academy.

The lunchroom was filled with police officers in civilian clothes.

The trainees do not eat in the public restaurant. Chief Vernon was greeted by many of the men, and he stopped to exchange pleasantries at several tables.

When we ordered, I said that I wanted to choose from the salad bar. The waitress told me it was at the other end of the restaurant, so Bob Vernon stood up and said, "I'll take you there." He led me briskly through three dining rooms to the counter with the salad ingredients.

I was dressed in my tailored best, complete with authoritative briefcase, the epitome of the career woman, and I was being led to the salad bar! I've traveled all over the world by myself, have been lost on most of the major freeways within a five-hundred-mile radius of my home, have led five tours to the Middle East, and here I was being gently, but firmly, propelled toward a pile of lettuce!

Okay, Bob Vernon, if you're ready to talk about "Who's in Charge Here," I'm ready to hear the principles.

Who knows what might have happened to the progression of this book if I had followed my own instincts and walked toward the target range?

C. C.

Who's in Charge Here?

I have a Siberian husky who was bred to pull sleds. When I run in the morning, I put a harness on her and she leads me through the streets of Pasadena at a fast pace. After she drags me home, she is panting in ecstasy, having performed the role she was born to fulfill.

When my beautiful wife presented me with each of our children, I'll never forget the expression of joy upon her face. She was happy in fulfilling her God-created role of bearing a child.

When a man is fulfilling his true masculine role, he feels good about himself. He has a positive self-image when he is accomplishing what he was directed to do. Many men, however, don't know what their roles are; they flounder in swamps of confusion. They are like a football player who doesn't know the location of the goalposts.

True happiness comes from the satisfaction of fulfilling our roles in life.

A Happy Cop

Police officers are a breed of men I know well. When a cop is doing his job, he's happy, although frequently he finds it's tough to know what he did that was constructive. In other jobs a man might see a wall that's a little higher than when he started, a house that has a roof on it, or an electronic structure that he engineered. In police work, the results are intangible.

Once in a while, however, a cop has a chance to interact with the victim of a crime. My first opportunity of this kind came when I was a smooth-faced rookie, just out of my training.

It was my first week in a radio car by myself. My district had a pretty high rate of stolen cars, so I had been told if I wanted to get a hot car, to hang around the high schools when classes let out in the afternoon. A lot of guys will drive up to the school to show off for their buddies. It's a matter of status to see who is driving the sharpest wheels.

I cruised by the high school on my beat and noticed this kid, who could barely see over the steering wheel, driving a car that had a broken side vent. The glass was still clinging to the side of the car. I figured it must have been broken for a reason, so I came up behind him and turned on my reds. He pulled over, and as I walked up to him he was so white I thought he was going to pass out. When I started to talk to him, I could immediately tell that the car was stolen: It was hot wired; there was no key in the ignition; and he didn't know the registered owner's name. I impounded the car and took the kid back to the station with me.

While the young car thief was being booked, I called the owner of the car. His wife answered the phone and said, "I'm sure it's a mistake. My husband is at work, and he has the car."

I called the owner's office and asked, "Do you have a white, fifty-four Chevrolet?" He said he did, and I said, "Well, I think I have it." "That's impossible," he answered. "It's right outside the shop in the street."

"I suggest you go look and see if it's there."

A few moments later, he was shouting into the phone, "It's gone. Someone stole my car!"

"Well, I have it, sir."

That man came down to the station and was very appreciative. "You got it before I knew it was gone!" He was so excited that he kept patting me on the back. "What a fantastic police department we have in this city. You're doing such a good job, for one so young."

I was just twenty-one, fresh out of the Academy. I was really proud to be fulfilling my role, to be doing what I was supposed to do. This citizen was paying me, through his taxes, to get his car back, and I did.

A Happy Man

Doing what God wants me to do as a man is the basis of a successful marriage and family life. If we are out of our roles as husbands, out of our true masculine role, we are going to have unhappy families.

This important concept is in Psalm 1; upon it hinges the source of happiness:

Oh, the joys of those who do not follow evil men's advice, who do not hang around with sinners, scoffing at the things of God. But they delight in doing *everything God wants them to,* and day and night are always meditating on his laws and thinking about ways to follow him more closely.

Psalms 1:1, 2, *italics mine*

What does God want me to do? How do I find the principles for that great marriage and good family life that I want so much? Very early in my police career I began to be interested in family relationships. The majority of the time I spent on the street was in juvenile work. I worked on narcotics and juvenile narcotics, and if I have any expertise in police work, that is where it is.

In my years in juvenile work, I noticed something about those individuals who were classified as juvenile delinquents: Over 90 percent of them came from what we would call problem homes. I wanted to know what were the root causes of this breakdown of the family, so I began to do some research and study, especially in the Scriptures.

A cop is pragmatic; he has to be, in order to survive. An untested theory may sound good, but, until it's tested, policemen shy away from it. In our business, an untested theory could cost a life. We don't like something that is just philosophically or theoretically correct; we want a workable plan.

I have found the principles in God's Word are practical; they work. There is an orderly aspect to these principles, which begins with a well-defined line of authority. God has established this chain of command for our benefit, to give us guidelines in what might otherwise be living in chaos.

As a law-and-order man, I am constantly discovering that the life within this line of authority is one filled with a sense of peace and fulfillment. When I rebel against this chain-of-command concept, the result is unrest and inner turmoil.

Line of Authority: Government

The first time I read the Bible's classic chapter that outlines our subjection to governing authorities, it sounded pretty radical to me.

> Everyone must submit himself to the governing authorities, for there is no authority except that which God has established. The authorities that exist have been established by God. Consequently, he who rebels against the authority is rebelling against what God has instituted, and those who do so will bring judgment on themselves.
>
> Romans 13:1, 2 NIV

Notice the passage doesn't give exceptions. It says there is *no* authority, except that which God has established. He has allowed even the bad governments to exist.

The big question is: What happens if the governing authorities tell you to do something contrary to what you know God wants you to do? For instance, during World War II there were men who committed atrocities on other human beings. Millions of people were slaughtered and gassed. During the trials which followed, part of the defense was, "I only did what I was ordered. When my superior officer told me to turn on the gas, I did it." The judgment at Nuremberg said that was no excuse; there is a time to reject the order of a superior.

A situation in the Bible helps me understand the application of the Nuremberg principle. God tells us to be in subjection to the governing authorities, and yet there were times when the apostles refused to obey that directive.

In the Book of Acts, Peter and John were preaching boldly. The governing authorities were angry and commanded them to cease teaching about Jesus. The leaders were a real power bloc; the senate and religious leaders were the civil, criminal, and religious authority combined.

Peter and his friends refused to comply with the stop order and consequently were whipped and sent to prison. Then an amazing thing happened: During the night, an angel of the Lord unlocked the prison gates; and, by sunrise, Peter and his pals were teaching in the temple again. What a shock the jailers must have had!

The captain of the temple guard brought his renegade prisoners before the Jerusalem Council again. This time he treated the apostles gently. If these guys could walk through locked doors, they could do anything!

The high priest said, "We gave you strict orders not to continue teaching in this name [the name of Jesus.]" But Peter and his friends answered with *the only valid reason for breaking the ruling law of the land:* "We must obey God rather than men" (*see* Acts 4:19, 20).

As a cop, I know a lot about authority and resistance to authority; this is the essence of my job. The Bible talks about policemen in Romans 13. It says that rulers, (the Phillips translation says "keepers of law and order") are not a cause of fear for good behavior, but for evil.

Have you ever been whizzing along the freeway, when suddenly you found yourself passing a black-and-white highway patrol car? What did you do? Instinctively, you applied the brakes; even if you were not speeding, you thought, *If I'm passing him, I must be going too fast.* I find myself looking at my speedometer when I pass another policeman. Am I within the speed limit?

The principle God has is:

> For rulers hold no terror for those who do right, but for those who do wrong. Do you want to be free from fear of the one in authority? Then do what is right and he will commend you. For he is God's servant to do you good. But if you do wrong, be afraid, for he does not bear the sword for nothing. . . .
>
> Romans 13:3–5 NIV

We don't have swords dangling from our belts today, but God thinks that submission to authority is so important that He has vested in government the responsibility to utilize deadly force, if necessary. Many times I've been asked how I, as a Christian, can bear arms. I wear a gun on my hip, because, in my chosen profession, the Bible gives me that right.

When I was considering a career, I had to wrestle with the commandment "thou shalt not kill." Should I be a policeman? Does that mean it is *never* right to kill? Well, I discovered that the word *kill* in the Book of Exodus is translated from a Hebrew word whose actual meaning is "murder." God has given us specific commands about murder, stealing, lying, sexual promiscuity, and other offenses, but in all areas that He hasn't covered specifically the government is in charge.

I've heard people say, "I don't think the Bible has anything to say about it; I know the government says to do this, but my conscience tells me I should do something else." I believe a person is on his own when he starts talking about *conscience.* The Bible says you will obey the government, if you can't find a specific command that says otherwise. This applies to income tax, laws, rules, and regulations, even if you do not agree with them.

There are many examples in the Bible of instances in which God worked through godless governments. He can work through the president, congress, the governor, even through those whose policies and politics we don't like. At the time Paul wrote the standards for obedience to the government, the rulers in Rome were tyrants. However, the apostle, under the inspiration of God, says, "Obey those guys."

This line of authority is emphasized when the Bible says: "Submit yourselves for the Lord's sake to every human institution: whether to a king as the one in authority, or to governors as sent by him for the punishment of evildoers ..." (1 Peter 2:13, 14 NAS).

Line of Authority: Your Boss

Another link in this chain is between "slaves and masters," (1 Peter 2:18 NIV), although we call them employees and employers today. The Bible says that while you are on the job you follow the instructions of your boss. This doesn't mean we should be carbon-copy yes-men, either. We need to express our opinions and give our bosses the benefit of our expertise. A sincerely loyal person will warn his boss if he sees danger in unwise decisions. Blind obedience is foolish, but once you have explained your viewpoint, and the boss understands, then it is up to you to obey his directive.

"Slaves [in modern times this should be interpreted as employees], be obedient to those who are your masters according to the flesh, with fear and trembling, in the sincerity of your heart, as to Christ" (Ephesians 6:5 NAS).

Whatever your job is, I think it is your responsibility to perform in the Spirit of Christ. This doesn't mean we should collar everyone in sight and witness to them. I know some Christian policemen who present the Gospel to their captive audiences in the back of a squad car or behind bars, whether their prisoners are receptive or not. Personally, I don't think this is appropriate. I believe God will give us many opportunities to share Christ, if we live as He wants us to live.

If you have been called into police work or to be a doctor or engineer or run a business, then that is what you're supposed to do while you are on the job. I believe in working sincerely, as an employee of Christ, but under the authority of your employer, during working hours. The Bible says: "And whatever you do in word or deed, do all in the name of the Lord Jesus, giving thanks through Him to God the Father" (Colossians 3:17 NAS).

I see no contradiction between obeying the governing authorities and following God's specific commandments. Something which happened with my children puts this into focus.

Bob and Pam are four years apart; by the time Pam was twelve years old, we decided we didn't need a baby-sitter anymore. When we would leave, we would tell Bob that Pam was in charge. He didn't like that, but most younger brothers don't. I would say, "Now, Bob, I want you to understand that you have to obey Pam when I leave you under her control. There are a couple of things I want you to do tonight. First, help Pam with the dishes, then go over your spelling words three times, and go to bed at nine o'clock. Got that? But Pam is in charge, don't forget."

What I really did was give Bob three specific commands. However, in the areas I didn't cover, Pam was to be in charge. What do you think would happen if we left, and then Pam said to Bob, "Dad said I'm in charge, so you can forget about going to bed at nine. I want you to stay up and watch *Frankenstein Meets the Wolf Man* with me."

What is Bobby to do when nine o'clock rolls around? What should he say when I come home and see him sitting in front of the TV, with his hair straight up, scared stiff? Should he say, "But, Dad, Pam was in charge, and she told me to stay up."

The two principles, the specific command and the authority in charge, do not contradict each other. We are to submit, obey, follow the line of authority God laid out for us, as long as there is no conflict with a specific command from God.

Authority in the Family

Who's in charge here? God has established His line of authority in family relationships. In one of the most misunderstood passages in the Bible, it says, "Wives, be subject to your own husbands, as to the Lord. For the husband is the head of the wife, as Christ also is the head of the church, He Himself being the Savior of the body" (Ephesians 5:22, 23 NAS).

The husband is the head of his wife; this relationship can be beautiful and harmonious or disjointed and tragic. Have you ever seen slow-motion pictures of a pro-football player going through the line or a gymnast performing on the bars? They have their bodies under the control of their heads. Their brains are thinking thoughts, and their bodies are reacting in perfect coordination. The head can't go without the body; the body can't function without a head.

On the other hand, it is a sad sight to see a body that is out of control. It is appropriate that God uses the example that a wife and husband are linked together as one unit. In a body, is the ear or the elbow or the finger any better than any other part? No, it's all one body. It works together. The Scriptures say that the body should follow the directions and be submissive to the head.

In the man-woman relationship, the Bible doesn't say that men are better than women or more qualified or superior, but it does say that in any arrangement where there is more than one person, there has to be submissiveness and authority.

God gives men some sober responsibilities in this arrangement. One of the main topics in this book will emphasize how men can fulfill God's intended role for them, so that their wives will want to be submissive to them.

The line of authority is a basic concept which is important to understand, even when it hurts. I remember one time when my boss made an arrangement with me that I didn't like. He called me into his office and asked me what my reaction was to his directive. I said, "Well, I view myself as a diamond in the rough, and you are the chisel. You're whacking away at me, and it hurts. But the polishing of that diamond will make me a better man."

I told my boss that God had placed him in authority over me, and it was God who was using him to chip away at me. This may have blown his mind a bit, but he appreciated that statement.

Our God is powerful. It doesn't take any effort on His part to put a thought in someone's mind of how to treat us. This is the security we can have in the line of authority relationships, whether it is a government official, a boss, a husband, or parents, God has it in His hands. If we are obeying and following this line of authority, He will honor it.

Submission is not slavery; it is the logical, practical, biblical way to live.

3

Some men seem to be naturally endowed with leadership abilities, but others learn the conditions of leadership by study and experience. I don't think leaders are born or made, but molded.

No one can assess a person in a position of leadership better than someone who has worked under him. I asked Sergeant Russ Malmgreen, a young man who had served for three years in Operations Central Bureau under Chief Vernon, "What leadership qualities does Vernon have?" Sergeant Malmgreen answered me so fast that I wished I had learned shorthand. He said, without hesitating between words, "Integrity, honesty, openness, receptivity to ideas, attentiveness when listening."

When the sergeant worked in Central, Bob Vernon had fifteen hundred people, including two commanders and six captains, under his command. However, Malmgreen has been transferred to another division since then, so his remarks to me about the chief were not apple-polishing the boss. He said, "Chief Vernon had an open-door policy—he was never so big that he wouldn't listen to your problems."

I asked the sergeant what Vernon was criticized for, and he answered, "Some of the guys said he was 'too religious,' but I'll tell you he wasn't self-righteous. He was tolerant of the views of others, but he never compromised his principles.

"You should have seen the guys who were really into the drinking, smoking, and swearing scene—they cleaned up their act around Chief Vernon. It wasn't because he ever said anything; it was just that they respected him as an individual.

"I grew under his direction. It was a fantastic experience."

C. C.

Why Follow Me?

I know men who say, "I'd like to be the head of my family, but my wife just takes over." What they are really saying is that their wives don't respect them.

How do we earn respect? By demanding it? How can we be leaders in our homes? Some men may be presidents of large companies or professionals who are respected in their communities, and yet their wives treat them like pieces of limp spaghetti. Other men keep their families cowering in fear of an impending explosion. Somewhere between the bowl of custard and the sledgehammer is the vast army of the uncertain, who aren't sure of themselves as leaders and yet aren't weak enough to be considered flaccid fellows.

A man may possess the character traits of a leader, but he also needs to fulfill certain conditions of leadership. Why should anyone play follow-the-leader? Because man was created for leadership and God can turn our mediocrity into excellence, if we are under His authority.

Man: The Leader

In Genesis, the Book of beginnings, it says that man was created to subdue and rule over all life. A man, to be fulfilling God's intended role, should be a leader.

"And God blessed them; and God said to them, 'Be fruitful and multiply, and fill the earth, and subdue it; and rule over the fish of the sea and over the birds of the sky, and over every living thing that moves on the earth' " (Genesis 1:28 NAS).

You're a man. You're in charge. You were created to be a leader.

Man was also created to rule over the woman. "To the woman He said, 'I will greatly multiply Your pain in childbirth, In pain you shall bring forth children; Yet your desire shall be for your husband, And he shall rule over you' " (Genesis 3:16 NAS).

Here is the second important principle for man: Not only is he to rule over the world and the animals and everything on earth, but also he is to rule over the woman.

There are two important words in that passage from Genesis. One is *desire*, and the other is *rule*. For a long time I thought that *desire* meant "sexual desire." However, my pastor, John Mac-Arthur, clarified this passage for us in a way that changed my understanding of the man-woman relationship. The original Hebrew word for *desire*, in this case, means "to control." In other words, the woman is going to try to control her husband, and the husband will want to rule over her. How true!

It wasn't always this way, however. When God created us, He made man and woman in complete harmony. Adam and Eve were given freedom of choice and chose to disobey God. Sin came into the world, and the perfect relationship between man and woman was split.

Without biblical principles, without God's guidance, the marriage relationship will be one of discord, disagreement, and disunity.

There you have it: man, woman, someone in charge. Today a lot of people don't believe that should be. They say, "Just let it happen." A couple may think they can both be the decision makers and everything will be fine. I think that's naive. Many times two people can live together and be in complete agreement, but once in a while someone has to say, "Wait a minute, this is what we should do."

Unless there is recognition of authority and submission to authority, there will be problems.

It sounds very free and acceptable to have an organization without rules. But someone has to make decisions. I heard an interview with a popular feminist leader who was talking about her magazine. She said that in the United States we suffer from the distorted idea that someone has to be in charge. On her magazine, she explained, no one is in charge: It just happens.

How can she believe that? Who decides what stories are going in each edition? Who decides what hours the employees are going to work and who gets paid what salary? Someone makes decisions in any organization.

If man is created to rule, then let's look at some of the credentials he needs for his role as leader.

A Leader Is Under Authority

The greatest leader in human history was Jesus Christ. His followers were a ragged bunch: uncertain, doubting, confused about their calling, vacillating in their commitment. They followed the Master because He was a man who spoke with authority. He was under the authority of the God of the universe; He was a leader who loved them and accepted their human stumbling. The disciples were not forced to follow Jesus; they went with Him of their own free wills.

Throughout the ages we have had presidents, leaders in industry and the arts, kings, and monarchs whose names are recorded in history books, who used power and position to establish their right to rule.

The role God intended for us as men, the type of leaders He wants us to be as husbands, is to be under authority ourselves. That authority comes from God.

I have seen the restlessness and uncertainty of men who do not know the source of that authority. Some are full of pride and bluster through every situation. Others find their authority in the jobs they hold or the university degrees they have or their family genealogies. None of these are lasting. The job can fold; the degree is only a piece of paper; and the black sheep in the family can cause a blight on the family tree.

In a world torn with uncertainty and filled with worthless pursuits, only those things that are permanent and unchanging have value.

God is logical; He gave us His logic of leadership when He said, "But I want you to understand that Christ is the head of every man, and the man is the head of a woman, and God is the head of Christ" (1 Corinthians 11:3 NAS).

The little band of disciples had trouble understanding this concept of authority. It is even more difficult for twentieth-century man to understand it.

A Leader Has a Servant's Heart

Some men may point at Genesis 3:16 and say to their wives, "See this? See what the Bible says? I'm to rule over you." There they stop, rule book in hand.

What kind of relationship does this mean? Should the man be overbearing? a dictator in his home? a rigid authoritarian? Not at all. Here is what the Bible means when it says we are to rule over our wives.

Jesus was talking to His disciples, who were having some difficulty understanding this concept of ruling:

> And calling them to Himself, Jesus said to them, "You know that those who are recognized as rulers of the Gentiles lord it over them; and their great men exercise authority over them. But it is not so among you, but whoever wishes to become great among you *shall be your servant.*
>
> Mark 10:42, 43 NAS, *italics mine*

This is the type of rulers or leaders we are to be: men with servants' hearts. Christ led by example; He led by loving His disciples. Ultimately, He led by giving His life for them.

This type of leader doesn't crack the whip, make unreasonable demands, or shout orders. He does not "lord it over them."

The other day I saw a bumper sticker which said, QUESTION AUTHORITY. I believe that speaks to the mood of our society today. Authority is viewed by many as an evil in itself. Perhaps this is because authority has been blatantly abused by some. When we see the results of battered wives and abused children, we know the concept of authority has been distorted.

However, authority is not an evil: It is a necessity. We can't live together without it.

Dr. Henry Brandt, a Christian psychiatrist, told me, "If wives are to submit to the leadership of their husbands, every husband has the responsibility of being the kind of man who warrants submission."

A Leader Is Loving

I don't expect my wife, Esther, to respect me or obey me because I tell her she should. I know that I must earn her respect, must try to be the kind of leader she wants to follow. It is my responsibility to be the man God intended me to be and to accomplish the role for which He created me.

Our responsibility flashes out of the Bible like a neon sign with ten-foot-high letters. "Husbands, love your wives, just as Christ also loved the church and gave Himself up for her" (Ephesians 5:25 NAS). Wives are told to obey us, follow us, and submit to us, but the only admonition we are given is *to love them*. It does not say to crack the whip or make them toe the mark; it says to love them.

I'm not a Greek scholar, but I do know that, in that verse, the word used to describe love is *agape*. The Greeks were very precise in the shades of meaning they gave to a word. I guess they would have thought the English language was pretty sloppy. *Agape* is the godly love; it is the love which is totally giving. It is the love that says, "I love you, not for what you do for me, not in return for the amount you love me, but I love you totally, sacrificially."

In the New Testament there are two other words for love: *eros*, the erotic or sexual type of love and *phileo*, the friendly, brotherly type of love. In a marriage, all three types of love may be present. *Eros* love is evident in its meaning. It is a result of *agape* love. *Phileo* love is the type of love a soldier has for his buddy or a policeman for his partner. This is an unusual relationship; I've learned to love some policemen in this *phileo* way.

A cop spends more time with a brother officer than he does with his wife. You sit in the same car with him eight hours a night, sometimes sixteen hours, depending on the action, and you go through unusual situations. It's a relationship that really doesn't exist between any other human beings, except guys who have been soldiers and fought in combat. Cops learn to depend on one another, to trust their lives to one another. I've tried to describe this to my wife, and she has a hard time understanding it. There have been two or three guys I've worked with for long periods of time, and I love them like brothers. That is the type of love that *phileo* communicates. I believe that, in this sense, your wife should be your best friend, not just your lover.

However, the love of a man for his wife is higher than *phileo*. It is more than brotherly love. It is the *agape* love, which is the type of love Christ showed when He died for us.

My minister told me about a man who came to him and said, "I think I've got a hangup."

The pastor thought he had heard about every hang-up known to man. "What is it?"

"I love my wife too much."

The minister put it to him straight. "Do you love your wife as much as God loved us and gave His Son for us?"

"No."

"Then you don't love her *enough!*"

God never has His concepts unbalanced. This relationship of submission and authority doesn't mean that one person is better or superior to another. It means that submission is balanced with *agape* love. When you have that relationship, you have a perfect relationship. You don't have the husband lording it over the wife; you have him loving her. As the wife is submitting to her husband, she is recognizing the logic of leadership, in God's line of authority.

A Leader Is Respected

Today there are many women who are confused over this whole idea of submission. I really don't blame them. If, however, they understood that God established this pattern, not as a punishment, but as a part of a magnificent and orderly plan for living, their attitudes would change. The Bible says that wives are to submit to their husbands and respect them. Men, as we respond to God's role, we will earn the respect of our wives.

The next line of logic is that we are to have authority over and command the respect of our children. The neon signs have been turned on again! The Bible speaks to husbands and fathers: "He must be one who manages his own household well, keeping his children under control with all dignity" (1 Timothy 3:4 NAS).

If we do not have the control and respect of our children, we are not fulfilling God's role for our lives. Socrates wrote something in 450 B.C. that sounds like today's newspaper. "If I could get to the highest place in Athens, I would lift up my voice and say, 'What mean ye, fellow citizens. That ye turn every stone to scrape wealth together and take so little care of your children to whom ye must one day relinquish all.' "

Socrates could have been speaking to many fathers I know. I remember one case in particular; we picked up a young fellow by the name of Wayne, from an exclusive suburb of Los Angeles. He had a brand new Stingray Corvette, and when we busted him he had several kilos of weed on him. We impounded the car, because it was involved in a crime. I looked at him, handcuffed and head hung down, and said, "You know, Wayne, you may lose your Stingray on account of this. The state may seize it."

He didn't seem very disturbed with that knowledge. "I don't care. The old man gave it to me."

If you don't earn the money to buy something, it doesn't carry much importance. "That machine is worth a lot of money, Wayne—must be eight or nine thousand dollars."

He shrugged, "So it's the old man's money. I don't care."

I could tell from the way he was talking that he didn't think much of his dad. I thought maybe he would open up to me, and I could help him. "Hey, what's with it between you and your dad?"

His eyes became hard, far too bitter for a kid of his age. "I don't even know the bum, so I don't know whether I like him or not."

I made a rather obvious statement: "I detect you don't like your dad." Wayne looked at me with that "dumb cop" attitude. I began to press the subject. "It appears to me that your dad must like you a little bit to give you that kind of car."

"That's his problem. He thinks he can buy anything, even my love. He's too busy for me; he's always been too busy. He's always tearing off somewhere in some jet, closing a big deal."

Wayne was taken into custody, and I called his dad. He came into the station, and, when he found out his son was going to jail for selling dope, he broke up. I found out the ironic reason that this man had worked so hard for his son, Wayne. He wanted to give his son everything that he couldn't have when he was young. He gave him money, cars, a special house, all kinds of material things most kids don't have. In fact, that was why he was working himself into a coronary. The father had had a couple of mild heart attacks and was on his way to a third one.

All of his efforts had only alienated him from his son. What the boy wanted was his dad, not his dad's money. It really taught me a lesson. Someday we are going to have to turn over all the money we have made to our children. We each need to ask ourselves, *What kind of person will inherit my wealth if I haven't spent any time with him?*

Some men are working so hard to make it to the top that, en route, they lose the most important possessions they have. They have so little time and energy left for their wives and children. Men are supposed to be managers in their homes; the basic principles of management training in industry are the same as those the Bible outlines for a man to fulfill in his home.

A Leader Sets Goals

Executives in leadership roles are told to be objective setters. The Bible says, "A wise man thinks ahead; a fool doesn't, and even brags about it!" (Proverbs 13:16). If a man is fulfilling God's role for himself—the manly role—he makes plans. He doesn't live impulsively from moment to moment, allowing time and money to slip recklessly through his fingers. Every man should be an executive in his home. The long-range planning, the goal setting, are part of the staff development in a family, as well as a business or profession.

If a man doesn't set the objectives for his family, who is going to do it? The Bible says, "Teach a child to choose the right path, and when he is older he will remain upon it" (Proverbs 22:6). As those who set objectives, we must teach our children to make the right decisions. This takes time and knowledge of certain principles.

A Leader Has Principles

As a manager, I have found it very important to spend at least two hours a week with each of my immediate subordinates. I set aside one day a week and try to spend an uninterrupted amount of time with them. We go over a principle each week. For instance, the principle for one week might be: A good boss takes less than his share of praise and more than his share of blame. Then we interact on the principle; I ask them if they know what it means. At the end of a session, I might say, "I want you to use that principle in your area and pass it on to your subordinates."

Principles, not impulsive actions, should be used in making decisions. In developing our children we are training our staff at home. They are a father's immediate subordinates. If we don't develop our children, who will? the schoolteachers? They do the best job they can, but it's our ultimate responsibility.

A Leader Is a Team Builder

Another condition of leadership is the ability to build a team. Today there are high-powered seminars being conducted around the country on this concept. Management consultants are hired to teach classes in this discipline for business and industry. In our families, team building is even more important. This doesn't mean, men, that we are to be autocrats, moving people around with whips, but it does mean leading so that we work together as an effective team.

I'm a football buff. A few years ago the football team at my alma mater was having problems. Some linemen were mad at some backfield men. They decided they wouldn't open the holes for them; this made the backfield look very weak. The team wasn't effective. The members of the team weren't committed to the same thing.

In a family, the man needs to lead the members as a team. We can't be going on divergent paths, with different value structures.

A married man is the respected head of his family when he is striving to accomplish these conditions of leadership. We need to look at ourselves, men, and determine if we are under the authority of God. Do we have servants' hearts or dictators' fists? Are we loving? Do we command, not demand, respect? Are we setting personal goals and helping the members of our family set goals? Are we building a team spirit in our family, so that we work together, not pull in opposite directions?

It looks like a tall order, but, men, we do not have to do it alone. Superman is an invention of a vivid imagination. I have never leaped over burning buildings or held up a collapsing bridge with one arm, but I know that "... I can do everything God asks me to with the help of Christ who gives me the strength and power" (Philippians 4:13).

4

When a woman asks another woman about her husband, it's difficult to disguise reactions. We can tell when the response is genuine or forced. It's one of those vagaries which men can't understand. Call it woman's intuition.

We began with the usual social amenities: "Where did you and Bob meet?" Esther Vernon told me of their high school-college romance, which began one evening in 1953 at the Moonlight Rollerway, a Pasadena roller-skating rink. I suppressed the desire to ask if Bob had her going in circles on that first date.

Then I pushed the visceral question, "What did you see in him?" Esther said she had the feeling she could trust his decisions. "He exuded confidence in himself, which gave me the confidence I needed."

Ask a woman about her husband's most outstanding quality, and she may hesitate for a while before she answers. Or she may not be able to think of any! I asked Esther, and she said, "When I first met Bob I was impressed because he didn't have to prove that he was a man. He was a gentle person, but not weak; decisive and yet very thoughtful. My first impression was lasting. Those qualities haven't changed."

And then she made the observation which answered all of my unexpressed questions. "I knew from the start that Bob was a man who was looking for God's will in his life."

My intuition told me that Esther Vernon was happy that she was a part of that will.

C. C.

What About
Her Rights?

Women's rights are a blazing issue today. The idea of a woman being in submission to her husband is an irritant which develops into a full-scale battle in the minds of many women. Is a woman shackled in a system where her individuality or freedom is restricted?

No one is completely free. When we live in a society of more than one human being, complete freedom would be chaos. Freedom has its limits; having restrictions upon individual freedoms actually increases our total freedom. Conversely, no restrictions results in a state of bondage.

One day in the life of this cop illustrates a concept which encompasses all rights in a free society. It's called optimum freedom. Optimum freedom tells us the point to which my individual freedom can extend before another's right to freedom is in danger. Perhaps this story will clarify optimum freedom for you, as it did for me.

A Chase in the Night

It was a dreary, overcast afternoon in Los Angeles. Beneath the gray skies, traffic was light across the Olympic Boulevard Bridge, but in a couple of hours cars traveling over that cement channel we call the Los Angeles River would be bumper-to-bumper.

My partner, Roy, and I decided to grab a quick cup of coffee before offices let out and the school kids hit the streets. Soon enough we'd have our hands full of calls for service. It was a good time to take five. We had just pulled into a fast-food stand when I heard the three familiar emergency beeps on our police radio.

Roy leaned forward and turned up the volume. "Here comes a hot one."

The voice of the hotshot operator punctuated the words: "All units on all frequencies stand by. Thirteen Adam forty-seven in pursuit. Give your location, thirteen A forty-seven, and describe the vehicle.

Over the radio, a siren screeched, and then the rapid, excited voice of an officer burst on. "Thirteen A forty-seven. We are pursuing a sixty-seven Pontiac, dark green, northbound on Central, crossing Jefferson."

"Thirteen A forty-seven, what is the vehicle wanted for?" asked the operator.

Once again, the siren announced another transmission from the pursuing unit. "Thirteen A forty-seven, we're still northbound on Central, approaching Adams—pursuing a sixty-seven Pontiac, Cal plate George Boy Union six five three. Will you give us a want warrant? All we have now is speed."

Central Avenue wasn't too far from where we were sitting, and they were coming toward us.

"Thirteen A forty-seven, come in." The hotshot operator was trying to get another location. The pursuing unit keyed open the mike, but there was no broadcast. I became increasingly tense. Then the cop's voice came in again. This time his tone was pitched even higher. "The vehicle we are pursing just T. A'd with a white Chevy at Central and Olympic; request ambulance and 'T' car be dispatched to that location."

"Thirteen A forty-seven, are you involved? George Boy Union six five three is stolen—occupants considered armed and dangerous."

"We're in pursuit now, eastbound on Olympic."

I shouted, "Hot dog, they're coming our way!"

We waited tensely. The stolen car was doing about eighty.

"Here they come," Roy shouted.

I could see three black and white police units, red lights ablaze, with a dark colored Pontiac out in front, leading the pack. Although they were a few blocks away, Roy punched the accelerator, and we leaped into the street. He was going to try to get out in front and slow the speeding car. We were at the head of this wild parade when I saw it happen. I had turned around to keep Roy appraised of the fugitive's position, when the front police car pulled up next to the Pontiac. The Pontiac veered suddenly into the path of that approaching black and white, then swerved to avoid a collision, jumped the curb, and smashed into a large, metal high-voltage-power pole. The pole sheered off at the base, crushing the entire front of the Pontiac. The car spun around twice, the wreckage coming to rest half on the sidewalk and half on the street. Glass, hubcaps, and metal debris showered the area.

Roy slammed on the brakes, and we skidded to a stop. He had seen the crash in the rearview mirror. We knew the Pontiac driver wasn't going anywhere. If he was alive, we knew he had to be seriously injured.

When we reached the wreckage we found that the occupant wasn't quite dead, but unconscious and bleeding badly. We called the ambulance while dozens of police officers maintained a wide perimeter around the downed power pole. It was high voltage, and there were several lines down.

It was beginning to get dark when we drove away from the scene of the wreck; we began to crawl with the traffic. At first I thought the jam was local, but, after several blocks at a snail's pace, we realized that this was the start of a hard night's work.

The power was off. The entire east side, blacked out. The sheared power pole was a main trunk line. A chain reaction was set off, which cut the current from lights; refrigerators; and, worst of all, traffic signals!

It was a real mess—traffic-jam city. Too bad the power didn't affect the car horns. I'll never forget that night; however, the experience did give me an appreciation for traffic signals. They are like your heart; you don't think much about them until they get fouled up or stop!

We had to direct traffic manually for several hours. Standing in the street, waving my arms, when motorists' tempers are short, is no fun. I really needed that cup of coffee.

Every police officer from the Hollenbeck station was deployed, plus several from three other areas. There weren't enough officers to handle the traffic, the questions, and the frayed nerves. I heard several stories that night of frustrated drivers who purposely rammed into another's car. A normal thirty- to forty-five minute drive home turned into a two- or three-hour nightmare.

Several hours later we pulled into the station parking lot. Everything was dark, which was unique, since police work never stops. As we walked in with a burglar we had picked up, I saw a strange sight: candles everywhere. I passed by the watch commander's office, where Sergeant Pistole was leaning over his desk, struggling to read through the arrest reports by the light of a cluster of three candles.

Roy and I finally sat down for that cup of coffee. He stirred the strong police-station brew and commented, "Bob, I learned one thing tonight. We need those crazy traffic signals out there."

Roy's words rang in my ears as I made my way home that night. At one intersection, I sat for a full minute, with only one car coming through from the opposite direction. Normally, I might get a little perturbed, needlessly waiting at a red signal and having my freedom restricted in that manner. However, I had learned an important principle that night: Restrictions upon our freedoms are for a purpose. Limiting freedom, like traffic signals, brings about order which actually increases everyone's freedom.

Don't Fence Me In

Many people are challenging the idea of restricted freedom, especially young people. They say, "It isn't wrong to do what I want, if it doesn't hurt anybody else." For instance, there is the matter of marijuana use. Some of us believe it is physically harmful; we know it changes a person's life-style. Some marijuana users develop the amotivational syndrome, which means they are not motivated to work and become dependent upon the rest of society; consequently, this takes away some of our freedom, because our tax bills increase. Even though marijuana users do not consider their habit immoral, the principle of optimum freedom says that their freedom is usurping some of my freedom.

In the world of business, the word *optimum* is frequently used in relation to company charts and graphs. If management determines that a certain amount of money should be invested in plant improvement, they often expect an increase in productivity. The company begins to add more manufacturing and office space, but there comes a point at which this capital outlay does not result in a corresponding increase in income. The ideal, from a management viewpoint, is to reach the optimum point in improvements and to avoid the point at which diminishing returns in productivity become evident.

The optimum point is the point of diminishing returns. You grant units of freedom to people, but when you get to a certain level, you reach that limit where freedom begins to erode.

Optimum freedom is misunderstood, and yet it is a critical topic in our society. How far can my individual freedom extend before another's rights are in peril?

Understanding optimum freedom encompasses all rights in a free society, including women's rights. It's part of a universal struggle.

Rights Versus Responsibilities

When a woman marries, her priorities are not the same as a young career gal without a husband or children. She has assumed a new role within the structure of society, and her life takes new directions. Certain restrictions within her life will produce better results in her marriage and her personal fullfillment.

The pastor of the church I attend gave a message, one Sunday, on the priorities of the woman. It didn't seem so startling at the time, since this is a Bible-believing and teaching church, and all he did was state what the Bible says. The women in attendance are, in general, committed Christians who are accustomed to hearing a solid hour of heavy Bible teaching every Sunday morning. However, that sermon caused a storm. There were some women who reacted so strongly that the story made the headlines of the *Los Angeles Times.*

Why? I believe this is an illustration of what a profound impact our total world-system values and present-day culture has upon our thinking. In many cases, what the Bible has to say on certain issues is so foreign and diametrically opposed to modern-day thinking that the ideas seem way out of line.

Within the women's liberation movement there is a great deal of propaganda that ridicules those who hold to biblical principles in regard to the role of a wife and mother. I've often heard the phrase, "Oh, you're just a housewife." Much of this propaganda is designed to take women out of the home and into more "fulfilling" roles. One of the leaders in the women's lib movement said, "The family must go; it oppresses and enslaves women."

Our current cultural climate is in opposition to some basic Bible statements. These biblical principles may be ridiculed or ignored, but they cannot be altered: ". . . encourage the young women to love their husbands, to love their children, to be sensible, pure, workers at home, kind, being subject to their own husbands, that the word of God may not be dishonored" (Titus 2:4, 5 NAS).

This principle agrees with a parallel passage in 1 Timothy 5:14 (NAS): "Therefore, I want younger widows to get married, bear children, keep house, and give the enemy no occasion for reproach."

Nowhere in the Bible do you find the *rights* of a woman or a man articulated, just the *responsibilities*.

Her Priorities

The priorities of a woman are: God, first; second to demonstrate her love for her husband; third, to raise children (not just *have* children, but to be responsible for their socialization); fourth, to be a worker at home.

Now, before every working woman becomes inflamed over these principles, let me say that the Bible doesn't say that once those priorities are fulfilled a woman must stay at home. On the contrary, Proverbs 31 is very specific in documenting a wide variety of roles that are proper for a woman to accomplish. There are enough duties and responsibilities in Proverbs 31 to keep any woman happy and satisfied, almost without limitations.

During the child-rearing years I believe a woman has a full-time task. However, I am aware of many women who do much outside the home, once the children are raised.

Inflation and our standard of living have made it almost necessary today for a supplemental income, which means the husband is either holding down two jobs, or the wife is assisting in bringing home money. What is occurring, in many cases, is that the family is putting material values over and above human values. When the point is reached when those material wants are placed above the healthy, emotional needs of the children, the problems come into families.

The question still hasn't been answered: What about the woman's rights? What about her interests? First of all, if we believe God is in control and if we trust that He is who He says He is, a woman who is submissive to her husband, a woman who is putting biblical priorities first, will be taken care of by the all-omnipotent God. There is an exception to this principle of submission discussed in chapter two.

Women are not to exercise authority over men, but to be submissive. The instructions are also given that ". . . [she] shall be preserved through the bearing of children . . ." (1 Timothy 2:15 NAS). For many years this didn't make sense to me, but as one begins to examine the context, it becomes very relevant.

What this is saying is that if you have a husband who is abusive, uncontrolled, unloving, undisciplined, his mother literally made him into the man he is. In God's economy, there is perfect balance. The woman must be submissive to the man, but the man is what he is because of the woman who raised him.

Womankind will have a powerful impact upon the type of men to whom they are to submit, through the fact that they bear the children. *They have the power to shape the character of the man to whom someday another woman must submit.* What an important job and what a beautiful balance!

In my opinion, the reason crime began to skyrocket in America around World War II is because women began to leave the home, and children had to fend for themselves. There is a direct relationship between juvenile delinquency and women working outside the home. I am against child-care centers. The best route is for the mother to raise and teach the children, rather than the state or some disinterested individual.

To some people, the priorities and responsibilities of a woman may seem restrictive. However, the end results can produce better marriages, happier children, and the welfare of our total society. And that means optimum freedom for everyone.

5

When I first met Bob Vernon he was Captain of the Venice Division of the LAPD. Venice, California, in the early 1970s was the center for strange cults, Satan worship, and bizarre behavior. I vividly recall that original interview. Vernon communicated some startling stories to me, some of them so gruesome in detail that they couldn't be included in the book I was writing with Hal Lindsey, *Satan Is Alive and Well on Planet Earth.*

When a man has a job with negative aspects, what happens when he goes home? Can he separate his work from his family life? Esther Vernon told me that Bob didn't relate what was going on in his police work, unless she wanted to know.

Communication, however, is more than hearing or repeating facts. Communication is conveying thoughts and feelings to others. We communicate with our eyes, with the tone of our voices, with body language. We communicate with silence.

When you meet the members of a man's family, you know how they feel toward one another. After a dinner in the home of the Vernons with son Bob, a husky college student, and daughter Pam, a nurse, and her husband, Steve, another police officer, it was quite obvious that they communicated well with one another. It didn't take an investigative reporter to see that their actions spoke louder than words.

Do you hear what I'm saying?

C. C.

What Did You Say?

If I don't communicate with you, nothing will happen. If I am able to communicate with you, ideas may be exchanged, friendships may be established, personal relationships built. Communication can open understanding or lock out agreement.

Marriages are destroyed or enhanced by negative or positive communication. Relationships between parents and kids are determined by the degree of communication they achieve together. Do these phrases sound familiar? "Talk to me." "Shut up!" "Look at me when you talk!" "It's not the words I hear, but the music." "I just can't understand what he's thinking!"

Since communication is so important, the principles of effective communication can be applied to every situation, especially in the home. One of the duties of the man, as the leader in his home, is to make sure people are talking to one another, and that he is talking to them. It is a continual responsibility to keep those lines open, to get the facts before he makes decisions, and to be attentive to the needs of people around him.

As a police officer I'm very aware of the value of good communication. We have a system we are developing in the department called the ECCCS (Emergency Command Control Center System). At the present time, we use a radio telephone operator, who dispatches a call to the closest unit. This consumes a great deal of valuable air time. The computer system will cut that dispatch time from several seconds to a fraction of a second, since messages will be sent in computer language.

When this system becomes totally operative, the message will be transmitted to a television set in the patrol cars. Another feature will be direct contact with our computer files. For instance, if a police officer stops a car and pulls a guy over for speeding, he can run his license number though the computer, and it will print out whether the speeder is wanted or not. If there's a warrant outstanding, if he's jumped bail, it would print that out, and the officer could take him to jail and book him.

This is an amazing advance in communication. We have a couple of police cars equipped this way, and it works.

Problems in Communication: Using Words

Communications have problems—not only sophisticated problems similar to our police department, but also person-to-person communications are complicated. Communication is an interchange of thoughts; it comes from the Latin word *communis,* which means "common." What we are really talking about is the fact that we have the same thoughts in common. We need to transmit thoughts from my gray matter to your gray matter. That's really tough to do, to get some thoughts from my head to your head.

Educator Mortimer Adler said, "Fifty percent success in the process of communication would be very good indeed." If only half of my thoughts can get to your thoughts, I'm doing well.

What really occurs when we communicate? We go through a system. I get a thought, and, in order to get that thought from my brain to your brain, I have to use some type of device. Somehow my thoughts must be transposed into symbols. These symbols are words that I speak, words or pictures I put on paper, or gestures. Right now I am selecting words to carry my thoughts to you. I am encoding, or putting my thoughts into a coded group of symbols. If we were talking, these symbols would be expressed in grunts and sound waves that go through the air. Your ear would pick up these vibrations, causing the air to carry different tone inflections. Then you would go through a system of interpreting what they mean. You decode that into your brain and say, "Oh, this is what he meant," and therefore form an opinion. We are lucky if we approach 50 percent understanding. When we have a good communicator and a person who knows how to listen or understand whatever medium we are using, then the percentage of understanding will be higher.

Let's do an experiment in problems of communication. Take out a pencil and paper and jot down the answers to these questions. If you are wearing a watch, put your hand over it and then tell me, how long you have had that watch. Describe it. What color are the hands? Are the numbers on the watch Arabic or Roman numerals? What is the color of the watch? What is the color of its face? Is there any writing on the face of the watch? Where is the writing, above or below the center of the watch? Is there anything else about the watch you can describe?

Now, bring your watch out and see how many observations you have which are correct. A survey provided by a research firm says that the average American looks at his watch sixty times a day. If you've had your watch for a few years, you can multiply and determine how many times you've looked at it. Most of the people I've done this experiment with get less than half the answers right. What occurs is that we go through a process of identifying something that is significant to us, and we filter out everything we consider unimportant. When you look at your watch, you're interested in the time. You're not too concerned about anything else. When we hear words, we have the ability to block out entire sentences which were insignificant to us.

I've tried to recount what has happened in a meeting, when another police officer will say, "Remember, Vernon, the chief said you should do this." I would say, "He didn't say that." I didn't want to hear it, so I didn't. I check with my secretary to see what she heard. "Did the chief say . . . ?" She just shrugs her shoulders and says, "He sure did." I had filtered it out.

We have problems with words. Is it any wonder that we have barriers in communication, especially in the family situation? The man is the leader, or executive, in the family. One of the prime roles of an executive is to be a good communicator. An executive spends about 75 percent of his time communicating. There are conscious and unconscious methods used in this process of communication. First, when we are encoding, we form the thought and choose the method we're going to use to transmit the message.

Sometimes that message is verbalized, sometimes it is communicated through the written word. Other times it may be shown through body language. Physical expressions and sounds from our mouths may be combined into effective communication.

What about the phrase "thanks a lot"? With the same words you may communicate sarcasm or appreciation. The expression on your face, your total mannerism, enters into this transmission of thought.

In the process of communication we also have decoding, which is the method of converting symbols to meanings and the meanings to thoughts. Our minds are complicated computers, and the processes of encoding and decoding are influenced by our attitudes.

We will consider some of the negative barriers to communication.

Feeling Threatened

Problems of communication begin with the attitude of the communicator. We reject threatening communication. If your wife or child comes in to talk and says something threatening, you may reject the entire conversation. You don't want to talk if you feel intimidated. For instance, what if your son says, "Hey, Dad, what's really wrong with premarital sex?" If you don't know how to handle that question, you will probably quickly terminate the conversation. You may retort, "If you don't know the answer, you'd better go back to kindergarten." You cut the communication, because you didn't want to talk about this subject.

I believe we have a problem in America today with the remnants of a Christian society. We live in the shadow of earlier values, with a lot of leftover rules that go along with the old Christian consensus. A few generations ago parents not only had rules, but they had reasons for those rules. They knew the principles upon which they based those rules and communicated these to their children. The children accepted the rules, because they understood the principles.

With the passing of time, the rules were repeated, without a discussion of the principle. When we get a question about premarital sex, a young person may have no knowledge of the principles. He just knows Dad said it was wrong, but he doesn't know why. Communication is severed, because many of us don't know the principles involved.

Thank God we can have the Scriptures to find those principles and not be threatened by communication.

Pride and Disinterest

Pride is another communication barrier. It can precipitate false communication. Selfish or ulterior motives, phony flattery, may propel us into saying things we don't mean, because we want something from the other person. This occurs frequently in business and happens a lot in the home.

Another attitude which is a problem in communication is disinterest on the part of the receiver. When wife wants to talk and husband is disinterested, watch out!

Recently I came home after dealing with a budget of $173 million for the Police Department. It had been reduced from $180 million. As I walked in from work, my mind whirling in millions, my wife said, "Bob, my checkbook doesn't balance." My mind was on millions. "Uh-huh, too bad."

"Bob, I've been over and over it, and I can't find the mistake." The amount that Esther couldn't find was $1.52. Big deal!

"Look, Esther, deposit a dollar fifty-two, or whatever else has to be done. I really don't care."

I did a good job of dampening communication by my indifference to Esther's concerns. We men may come home and find it difficult to shift gears and recognize that we are entering a different world.

One of the things that I see breaking up marriages and causing real problems in communication is this lack of appreciation for each other's worlds. We filter out everything except what is important to us. What the wife is concerned about is unimportant to the husband. She isn't thinking about $173 million; it's only $1.52.

To further complicate communication, along comes a child, whose sphere of activity is entirely unrelated to my problem as a police officer or my wife's role as a homemaker. He talks about something which is even less important to us. "Daddy, I lost one of my tennis balls today." First it's millions, then $1.52, then a tennis ball. I must learn the significance of these events in the lives of others.

I don't know why it is, but young people can detect disinterest more than older people, even more than your wife. In the ages from about ten to eighteen, they are very insecure, trying to find themselves and figure out what kind of persons they're going to be. They are very conscious of acceptance and interested in reading your thoughts and attitudes when they are talking to you. They can pick up a little turn of the head or raising of the eyebrows. If you're not interested in their problems, they're not going to bring any problems to you.

Jumping to conclusions is another problem which inhibits communication. You make your own interpretation, and you're not interested in letting the other person explain his view.

For example, your daughter comes home and wants to tell you about the problems she is having at school. She is anxious to tell you about her Spanish teacher. "Daddy, the teacher in the Spanish class gave us this test. . . ." Before she says another word, you're right in there. "I know, you probably think the test was too hard."

"Well, no, not exactly. You see this test was about conjugation of verbs."

"I get it. She didn't tell you how to conjugate the verbs ahead of time."

"No, she did that."

Have you ever talked to anybody like that? He won't let you finish what you're saying before he jumps to conclusions. Communication is blocked.

It's All in the Way You Look at It

Communication becomes more difficult because we interpret what we read and hear through our personal background of experience. When a word or an idea hits us, we try to relate it to something that will give it meaning. We will arrive at different interpretations, but, most important, with different attitudes.

If I should mention the word *Republican* to you, some of you would feel good about the word, others would feel indifferent.

Some might react with distaste. We would have different reactions to the word, because of experiences and knowledge we have.

Dr. William Haney, in his book *Communication and Organizational Behavior*, explains that we not only jump to wrong conclusions, or interpret words and thoughts differently, but we sometimes talk and think we're communicating, when we are really bypassing. Words really don't have meaning, but people have meaning; when we use words to try to get that meaning across to another person, we may bypass their understanding and not communicate at all. Bypassing is communicating on parallel lines.

In the Chicago area I became involved in a conversation with a local policeman. I introduced myself as an Los Angeles cop. We began to exchange some thoughts about procedures and I said, "In Los Angeles when that happens, we make out a shake card on the guy."

The local cop said, "When you shake someone down you write a card on it?"

"Sure," I answered, "we turn it in with our log."

"You mean you document that kind of action?" He seemed quite amazed.

"Of course, we record what we're doing."

"But couldn't you get in trouble for that?"

I couldn't understand this guy. He was asking me dumb questions.

He shook his head. "You mean you Los Angeles cops shake people down—right?"

I began to think these local cops were really dense. "Of course we do."

"I kind of figured you guys did, even though 'Adam Twelve' doesn't show it. You actually make a record when you shake someone down? I can't believe it."

I thought we were communicating, but we were on parallel lines. What he meant by "shaking someone down" was entirely different from what I meant. To a Los Angeles cop, shaking someone is writing a shake card or an F.I., as we call them. This simply means to stop someone to see what they're doing. If you're in a high burglary area and see a car that fits the description of one that's being used in burglaries, you shake them. You stop them and say,

"Hi, what are you doing here? Do you live here?" That's a shake, to a Los Angeles cop.

To a Chicago policeman *shaking* means something entirely different. A police officer may stop someone for going through a red light and say, "Now do you want a ticket, or do you want to handle this?" The guy hands a ten-dollar bill, hidden behind his license, to the officer, and he passes back the license, minus the ten bucks.

When the Chicago policeman said, "Do you document that?" and I said, "Of course," we were not communicating, we were bypassing.

My Mind Is Made Up

Another communication barrier is raised when we are dogmatic about our positions. We go through a process in which we abstract what we know about a subject and assume that's all you can know. We are all guilty of this at one time or another. It happens when your wife begins talking about something with which you disagree, so you determine you're not going to listen to her.

We need to hear other people's viewpoints. In police work there are many situations in which it's important not to jump to conclusions. We graphically illustrate this in police training. A picture is flashed on a screen, showing a group of people and a crime that has just occurred. Someone is on the floor, with blood running all over, and one of the suspects in the picture has a razor in his hand, another has a pistol. Some of the people are male and some female. There are different races and nationalities involved: a Negro, a Mexican-American, and a Caucasian. After having the picture on the screen for a period of time, we turn off the projector and ask various people in the class to describe what was happening. In the description, somehow the razor is placed in the Negro's hand, instead of in the Caucasian's. In reality, the Anglo had the razor. Why do you think the razor was reported in the Negro's hand? Because people's minds put it there. They stereotype, or abstract. We know it all; even though our eyes have told us something different, we don't accept it. What is being communicated to us doesn't make sense, so we block it out.

This is one of the things we try to indicate to the officers at our

Police Academy. We're going to have to recognize that we have prejudices and do our best to eliminate them.

These are some of the problems of communication. How can we solve them? How do we get thoughts from brain to brain, from person to person, from husband to wife, from parent to child, with all these problems?

The greatest Book of communication gives us the principles to break communication barriers. It speaks to us, so we may speak to others.

6

Some of us have learned to talk—too much. That small appendage inside our mouths can cause more trouble than any other part of the body. We sometimes want to bite it, and, in times of self-reproach, we may want to cut it out.

After we have hurdled some of the barriers to communication, how do we learn to communicate with understanding and sympathy to those around us?

"Look, I talk to the kids, and they're deaf. I talk to my husband, and he stares through and around me. Nobody ever listens to me!"

"I tried to talk to my teacher, but he didn't seem to hear what I was saying."

"I've explained over and over again to my wife, but she can't seem to understand!"

There's a proverb which says, "The tongue of the wise makes knowledge acceptable."

The first time I heard Bob Vernon speak, he took a subject which is full of controversy, especially coming from a cop. The topic was capital punishment. In the church that morning, crammed with several thousand people, he gave one of the clearest explanations for belief in capital punishment that I had ever heard.

However, better proof of communication skill came, not from the platform or the pulpit, but when Bob, Jr., said to me, "Dad is easy to talk to. We never kept any secrets from each other."

The most valuable audience is inside the home.

I wonder: If talk is so cheap, why do we make such costly mistakes?

C. C.

Let's Talk It Over

"A fool thinks he needs no advice, but a wise man listens to others" (Proverbs 12:15). Many of us are not accustomed to listening to others, because we are too busy listening to the newscaster, the comedian, the sportscaster, or the weatherman. We hear traffic and music, but need to learn the marvelous art of listening to our wives and children.

Listening Devices

Listening involves, first, trying to get inside the speaker and appreciate his viewpoint. If you're talking to a teenager on a high-school campus, try to recognize who he is and remember what it was like when you were that age. Realize the realities of life today in high school. How are you going to know, unless you listen to what he is saying? What is he trying to communicate? How would you view a situation, if you were in his tennis shoes?

Next, listen for total meaning. Try to pick up on the feelings that are being communicated by the person. A parent told me, "My little boy will come to me and say, 'Daddy, Daddy,' and won't say anything else until I *look* at him." Did you ever have a little one poke you until you gave him your undivided attention? You need to *look* at people when they talk.

The most important principle for being a good listener is to test for understanding. When communications are important, we use the feedback technique.

For instance, a boy said to me, "My dad bugs me."

"You mean your dad doesn't pay attention to you?"

"No, he pays attention all right, but he just bugs me."

"Are you saying there's something you do that he doesn't like?"

"I suppose so. It's this way; he has a drink or two before dinner, see, but he threw a fit when he found out I was smoking pot. Now what's the difference, I ask you?"

"Oh, so your dad is bugging you about pot?"

"Yeah, that's what I said."

Developing feedback is repeating what a person has said in another way.

A person will send out a psychological feeler by making a statement or asking a question. What he is trying to find out is whether or not you're ready to listen.

You arrive home after work and your wife says, "I have the worst headache!" Then she watches you. What she is asking is, "Are you ready to listen to my problems?" She really wants you to say, "Why a headache? Did something happen?" Now you've told her that you're ready to listen to her, and you will begin to communicate. What she wanted was to ask your advice, your counsel, or get some sympathy from you. That's called a psychological feeler.

Test for the meaning; demonstrate an interest. I think one of the best ways to show interest is to do something that person likes to do. Sometimes you can demonstrate interest by just sitting down and looking at him.

My daughter's bedroom was on the second floor of our house, and my bedroom is on the main floor. Just walking upstairs and sitting on the edge of her bed told her, "Pam, I'm interested in you. I'm willing to spend some time up here. Do you have anything to talk about?" I don't have to say it; just being there says I'm interested.

When Bob was younger, he loved to play basketball. I put a hoop above the garage for him. He knew that I didn't dig basketball; football was my game. However, when I played with him, he knew I was interested in him. When I came home from work, I'd see this preadolescent kid of mine kicking the dirt near the driveway. I would give him a pat on the shoulder and ask, "Hi, Bob, how are things?"

"Oh, they're okay."

"Anything interesting happen today?"

"Nope."

After I'd changed my clothes, I'd ask him if he wanted to shoot a few baskets before dinner. About fifteen minutes into the game, the same kid who had said earlier that nothing happened today, said, "I got into a fight today." Then he proceeded to tell me about knocking a kid over the seat of the bus, breaking a window, and tearing the kid's coat. Now that was nice to know, because sooner or later an angry parent would probably be making a phone call.

When I did something with him, like playing basketball, he knew that I was interested in him. He was probably thinking, *Dad's out there. He's ready to listen to me.*

A Communication Pattern

Dr. Ralph Byron is chief surgeon at City of Hope Hospital. He is a very busy man, but he told me one day, "It's important for me to establish communication patterns; I can't let it happen by chance. One little gimmick I use, Bob, that you may want to use, is pretty simple. I have a rocking chair that I call my communication chair. I tell Dorothy that when I'm sitting in that chair, it means that I want to communicate; I'm ready to listen. If I sit in the easy chair, I'm not ready yet. I need to unwind a little bit from surgery. But as soon as I move over to that rocker, I'm ready."

Dr. Byron has established a communication pattern. For a number of reasons, this is an important concept. For instance, I don't like to talk about heavy things before I go to sleep. When I went into the bedroom and started getting ready for bed, and Esther would toss some serious concerns on me, I'd turn her off quickly. I wasn't conscious of it, until I began to realize that I was violating all of the principles I teach. I wasn't listening to her. One night I said, "Honey, I really don't like to talk about heavy subjects before I go to bed, but let me give you some other times during the day when we can talk."

I have a rather unusual job, so I'm never sure when I will arrive home at night. Esther doesn't worry if she has dinner ready at five, and I don't get in until seven. Consequently, dinner isn't sitting on the table when I get home. We usually have around fifteen minutes from the time I walk in the door until I sit down and eat. So we have a little pattern. We have a breakfast bar by the island where Esther uses a chopping board to prepare salad fixings. I sit at the bar, and she knows this is my communication center. I'm ready to listen. We handle all kinds of home business for about fifteen minutes before dinner. It's a regular pattern.

I think it's important for men to establish habit patterns with their wives and children. When our kids were very young, we would play a game called "answer man." Every Tuesday and Thursday night was reserved for this, and they loved it. They would brighten up and say, "Dad, it's Tuesday night—answer man!" Both of them would have about four questions. Some of them were pretty strange. "How does God make snow?" "What makes wheels go around?" It was a game for them, and they tried to outdo each other with questions.

It became very natural that, when they got older, the Tuesday-and Thursday-night routines were established. At a time when they were becoming interested in knowing what was going on in life, it was natural for them to ask questions about everything—even sex. It was a habit pattern, a reflex action that really worked.

Honest Injun

In communication we not only need to learn to be good listeners, but to be honest. Communication is really inhibited when a person is known to be unreliable. "A good man hates lies; wicked men lie constantly and come to shame" (Proverbs 13:5).

People appreciate frankness more than flattery. That is a biblical principle from Proverbs 28:23. Honesty and frankness, however, need to be counterbalanced with this next great principle. "Some people like to make cutting remarks, but the words of the wise soothe and heal" (Proverbs 12:18). The true test of constructive criticism is to leave a person feeling he's been helped. If a person is saying, "Hey, this guy is a friend. I'm going to be a better person because of what he said," then the biblical principle of honesty is being used.

We can be frank without being cutting. There's a difference. I don't believe in sensitivity training in which you slice people apart.

I attended a sensitivity session during my master's program, in which we were locked up for a weekend together. There were some drastic results; it was like a pack of dogs, tearing one another apart. One person would be the victim, and the whole group would zero in on him with "frank criticism." One girl went to pieces and had to leave.

In this sensitivity-training session I saw people who were enjoying the cutting remarks. They were seeing how they could hurt. When someone said, "I don't like the way you comb your hair, or the dumb way you smile," or whatever stabs were being made, you could see the other person being emotionally destroyed by the person who was not being constructive.

I don't think that is what the Bible is talking about. Biblical frankness heals; it is soothing, not cutting. It's not critical, but helpful. ". . . Reliable communication permits progress." That's exactly what it says in Proverbs 13:17. We won't make progress if communication doesn't come across. If our children are afraid to talk to us because we shut them off, we'll never get anywhere in our relationship with them.

To be honest but constructive, we can phrase negatives in a positive way. I might say to my son, "Hey, Bob, I've noticed that you've made some improvement in following directions about taking out the trash. You can improve, but you're a lot better than you were two months ago." What did I do? I let him know that I wasn't satisfied yet, but recognized the success he has had. Now he has some encouragement.

Get Your Feelings in the Open

Every great man I know is able to accept criticism, to get unpopular feelings out in the open. The principle is: "If you profit from constructive criticism you will be elected to the wise men's hall of fame. But to reject criticism is to harm yourself and your own best interests" (Proverbs 15:31, 32).

You hear parents say, "I don't want to hear that in my house. I don't want to talk about it." What is the private reaction of that son or daugher? "Okay, I won't talk about it in the house." The feelings haven't changed; now they're seething underneath. It's the iceberg floating with nine-tenths beneath the surface, waiting to ram your ship. It is best to get that iceberg up on the surface, where you can melt it, or at least deal with it.

A few years ago my son was starting to listen to music by a popular recording star who used references to sex and perversion in his lyrics. My tolerance level was zero when I said, "I don't want to hear that stuff anymore. I dislike his music and what the words say. I don't want it in my house, understand?"

So what happened? Bob continued to listen to the same records when I wasn't around. We didn't have a chance to get our feelings in the open, and I didn't explain why I was so adamant about this particular music. Great exponent of principles I was!

I thought, *Vernon, you goofed. You shut off your boy, so that he'll never talk to you again, unless you make amends.*

I went back to Bob with an apologetic attitude. "Hey, I'm sorry for blowing my cool. Let's talk about this."

"You're sure you won't get mad, Dad?" He had a right to question my reactions.

"No, I really won't get mad, Bob."

"Okay, let's talk about it."

I asked him to get the evidence, which was the album in question. I pointed out some words to him and asked him if he knew what they meant. "Do you know what this is saying, Bob?"

"Golly, I never looked at it like that before. It's talking about lesbians, isn't it?"

He got the point. "Do you want these words bombarding your mind over and over again?"

The iceberg was beginning to surface. We came to a compromise. He agreed that there were certain songs by the artist that he didn't want in the house, and I agreed that there were other songs that weren't that bad. He understood why I disliked some of the music, and I understood why he liked some of the other pieces. I'm convinced that if we hadn't pulled our feelings out in the open, he would still be listening to the songs with bad connotations.

The words in some of the music today have a subliminal impact. It's similar to the tests which were conducted in a movie theater. They flashed the word *popcorn* on the screen for a ninetieth of a second; simultaneously a picture of butter dripping on popcorn was shown. It was so fast that the audience scarcely knew they had seen it, but their minds recorded the image. Popcorn sales went up. Our subconscious influences us more than our conscious. In the same manner, when words in certain songs repeatedly bombard us, we are subliminally getting the message. This is what I was trying to communicate to Bob.

Application of Principles

In the principles of listening, hearing the total meaning, being honest, and getting feelings into the open, there is a need for guidance. *Guidance* means "to show, watch over, to lead, to influence conduct, or to instruct."

To guide our children in the principles of successful living, we should be aware of their interests, their friends, their property, and their time. Without these elements no guidance through communication can be helpful.

An incident from my childhood has remained vivid throughout the years, because of my father's guidance. He knew me so well: my interests, my friends, my property, and my time.

I brought my bike home one day with a new fifteen-cent reflector unit on it. My dad was so aware of my property that he recognized something different and asked me where I got the new reflector. "From Donald," I answered. Dad asked the next logical question, "Where did Donald get it?" I was quick to answer, "He stole it."

I was seven years old at the time, and, as far as I was concerned, I was clean. *I* didn't steal it. However, my dad didn't see it quite the same way. "You have a stolen reflector on your bike?" Now I had already told him that, so I couldn't understand the big deal.

"Dad, I didn't steal it. Donald stole it. I didn't tell him to steal it. He brought it to me after he stole it, so I didn't have anything to do with it."

My dad was a big man. When I was seven, he looked like a giant to me. He looked way down at me and said, "Don't you understand how wrong it is to have stolen property?"

"No, sir."

"Bob, come out in the back."

I knew what that meant. In back of the garage was an apricot tree that he used for switches, and I usually got the swift end of one of them. This day he really surprised me. We sat on the orange crates, and he said, "I want to talk this over with you." We talked for at least forty-five minutes. This was my dad's day off, and he was a cop who got off five days a month. Those days were very important to him.

The branches of the apricot tree were intact, which made me a little more comfortable. Dad looked straight at me and said, "Bob, what's the name of the kid up the street? The one I'm always picking up."

"You mean Stanley?"

"Let's say Stanley comes over and rips off your reflector—no, let's use something else—say your sheepskin seat."

That didn't sound so hot to me, but I'd go along with the story, as long as I was still sitting down.

Dad went on with his "supposin'." "Then, Bob, Stanley takes the sheepskin seat and gives it to your best buddy, Albert Casino, and Albert puts it on his bike. A few days later you notice that Albert, your buddy, has your sheepskin seat."

"That dirty rat." Now I was mad at Albert. "He's no friend of mine."

Dad said, "Why? He didn't steal it."

It took a long time for a seven-year-old to understand the concepts involved in property rights, but by the end of that long talk I started to agree with my dad that it was wrong for me to have the stolen reflector. I said, "Hey, I want to give it back to the guy who owns it."

We got into Dad's car and drove over to Homer Street, where Donald lived, and returned the reflector to him. After that was over, Dad took me to the Sears bike department and said, "Now, you pick out any reflector you want. You've been honest, and you've done as much as you can to return what didn't belong to you. I want to let you know that I really appreciate your talking with me about this."

I picked out a great big fifty-cent reflector.

That was guidance, which is a lot different from rules. He could have said, "Receiving stolen property. Four eight six penal code section," and then reached for the switch and given me a few swats. I would have thought, *Hey, this is wrong. I didn't steal it, and I'm getting whipped for doing something I didn't do.*

The Bible says, "... fathers, do not provoke your children to anger ..." (Ephesians 6:4 NAS), and I would have been mad at my dad, because I didn't understand what I had done wrong. The next time I would have been more careful. If he asked me where I got something I knew was stolen, I probably would have said, "I found it."

I don't believe in rules as much as I do in principles. If we understand principles and communicate them to our children and our wives, the communication bonds will become stronger. We resort to rules, rather than guidance, because it takes more time to give guidance. It took my dad about three and a half hours to instruct me about stolen property. He poured that time of his life into a little seven-year-old boy and I've never forgotten it.

My father led by example. Did you ever try to push a string? You can't do it; you must drag it. The life that is following you can't be pushed ahead of you. Show me a young person who has a filthy mouth, and in most cases I'll show you a home where there has been a lot of profanity. My son told me one day, "As far as I know, I've never sworn." This was gratuitous information. I said, "That's really neat, Bob. I'm proud of you." He answered, "You know what, Dad? I've never heard you or Mom swear."

I realized the importance of what he said. Just to balance that out, I am not Mr. Clean, never making a mistake. I've seen my son do some things that are wrong, and as I've looked into my life, the reason he's done them is usually because he's seen me do the same thing.

It's not hard to be the kind of example we should be: It's impossible! We need outside help. That's what Christianity is all about. Having Christ in your life will give you the strength to carry out His guidance. It's the difference between rules and principles. I think that the rules we have, especially when a child is young, should be very firm. Small children can't understand principles.

There are two theories about rules: Some say they should be restrictive, and others say you should make rules broad. The problem with making rules too narrow is that you have to make a lot of exceptions, and that's a bad principle. I think it's important to have rules broad enough so that there is opportunity to move around, but when the line is there, you know there are no holes in it. The boundaries are clearly defined.

We used to have a correctional school in Los Angeles called Jacob Riis. If you had a problem in school or were kicked out of a school, you would be sent to Riis. I remember, as a juvenile officer, going into Riis to pick up some kid who had robbed a busman of his money and his watch. I went in to the principal, and he called in the boy and said, "Okay, where's the watch?" The youngster was defiant, "What watch, man?" Mr. Vandruff, the principal, said, "You know my rules around here, right? When I tell you I'm going to do something, do I ever fail to follow through?"

"No, Mr. Van."

"Then where is the watch?"

This time the kid didn't hesitate. "It's out in the alley, sir."

Mr. Vandruff didn't have to do anything, but soon I found out the reason. While I was there, the assistant principal brought a student into the office and said, "Three for him." Vandruff said, "Reach down and grab the handles."

The boy bent over and took hold of two handles that were bolted to the wall. Mr. Vandruff went over to his desk, brought out a belt, and whacked him. When he was through with this ritual, he said, "Look, Joe, what did I tell you when you were in here the other day?" Joe answered, "When I was late yesterday, you gave me two, and you said if I was late tomorrow I'd get three."

The principal continued, "Guess what happens if you're late tomorrow?"

"Whatever you say, I'll get," the boy quickly replied.

"Joe, I want to ask you a question," Vandruff spoke firmly, but not harshly. "I think there's a reason you're late, and you're not telling me. What is it?"

The kid shuffled around with tears in his eyes and said, " 'Cause we don't have a clock, that's why."

Vandruff called his assistant and said, "Put him on the list."

I wondered why this kid was put on a list for not having a clock, so I asked, "What list?" Vandruff shrugged, "Oh, it's the guys I wake up in the morning."

Then his assistant said, "Do you know what this guy does? In his own car, with his own gas, he wakes up about thirty-five guys every morning. These are kids whose parents either won't get a clock or won't wake them up. He helps them get to school on time."

I thought, *Wow, what a balance.* This is firmness underscored with love. That guy loved those kids so much, that he would wake them up, yet his rules were firm. I noticed that in Jacob Riis High School a lot of kids who started there were emotionally disturbed, very antisocial in their behavior, but after they were there for a while, they become calmer and easier to handle. They started to recognize that there really are boundaries. I think before they went to Riis they were testing to see where the boundaries were, and since they couldn't find any, they kept on going. After they got to Riis and met Mr. Vandruff, they saw where the line was drawn.

When young people are growing up, they don't always understand the principles. They do understand discipline, however, which is based upon the principles that prepare children for freedom. Layer upon layer of experience prepares them for adult responsibility.

We must be very careful about the experiences we put into the great computer God has given us. The GIGO Principle is computer talk for "garbage in, garbage out." Whatever you put into the computer comes out, so you can't blame the computer. Our minds are like that. The Bible says that what a man thinks in his heart, so he is. The thoughts that go into our minds program us.

Men, as leaders we have the responsibility of watching what kind of garbage enters our homes. The subliminal impact is very dangerous. We live in a hostile environment, and communication is a very important concept.

Probably the cause of most misunderstandings and the inability to get along within our families is that we don't use the principles from God's Word in daily practice.

Considering the chaos of a home without communication, do you think it's important to know those principles? I do.

7

Within the past few years, the Christian bookstores have been inundated with volumes on a subject that was previously allocated to secular circles. With sex being granted the acceptability it deserves, everyone seems to be writing about it.

I realized that Bob Vernon wasn't going to print an instruction manual, but when the subject matter for this chapter was discussed, I thought, *So what's new?*

While I was working on this chapter, our eighteen-year-old son came into my study with a couple of his friends. They sprawled on the old, plaid easy chairs and asked, "What's cookin'?" That question from healthy college kids usually should be taken literally. This time I had a swift answer. "Have you heard about the ice-machine concept?"

I gave them Vernon's illustration about the ice machine and had their complete attention. In a few moments I had answered my own mental question about what is new. Better yet, it was a natural and easy opening to talk with these young men about that old subject. It gave them food for thought.

C. C.

Sex—Alive and Well

Sex can be a great blessing or an incredible curse. It can be a source of tremendous satisfaction or a tool that causes deterioration and destruction. The Bible says sex is good; it is created by God, within His structure and with His guidelines. However, good elements can be warped and turned into bad.

In many ways sex is like an automobile. Before you think I've flipped, look at it this way. One weekend we went up to our cabin at Hume Lake, in the Sierras. We jumped into our car, with stereo multiplex, air-conditioning, and tilt seats, and took off in comfort, listening to music all the way. Not many years ago it would have taken days to get to Hume Lake; hours and blisters later, we would have arrived on horseback. It would have been a major project. A car is a beautiful invention when we use it to go to the Hume Chapel and hear good preaching, enjoy Christian fellowship, and do some rigorous dirt-bike riding. We had a wonderful time, due mainly to the invention of the car.

But I remember another experience with a car. I was a watch commander in the action-investigation division, when one of the sergeants phoned me and said, "Hey, we've got a multiple accident. It's a pretty bad one; I think you should see it."

I ran to my car, turned on the siren, and raced to the Harbour Freeway. A gal in a Thunderbird, doing about eighty-five miles an hour, had crashed into the rear of a station wagon full of navy officers' wives. It hit with such force that the wagon flipped over three or four times and ruptured the gas tank, igniting it. All six of those wives were cremated. When we finally gathered all the husbands together, we had to try to figure out which body belonged to which husband. I saw a lot of men come apart completely, trying to make an identification.

The experience was horrible. I can still smell the gruesome odors surrounding those cars. The automobile can be a terrible weapon of destruction. The gal driving the Thunderbird was loaded on six Nembutal capsules and didn't know what she was doing. She abused the car.

In Christian circles, the idea of sex being bad or nasty exists because we see so much of its abuse in our culture today. Instead of a beautiful trip with stereo music, we see the car hitting the station wagon.

God didn't intend sex to be bad. He created man and woman in His own image, blessed them, and said "be fruitful and multiply." To multiply, there has to be sex involved. God saw all that He had made and, "Behold, it was very good."

Since God made man and woman, it only makes sense to consult Him to get the most out of this relationship.

Principle Number One: Sex Is Good

God says that sex should be an integral part of marriage. It is part of His plan that husbands and wives have rights to each other's bodies. "The wife does not have authority over her own body, but the husband does; and likewise also the husband does not have authority over his own body, but the wife does" (1 Corinthians 7:4 NAS). The next passage says a very interesting thing about sex: *Don't deprive one another.* You can agree, for a limited time, to be apart, but don't stay away too long, for Satan will tempt you.

If sex were wrong, would God be saying that it's beautiful and not to deny or deprive each other of this fantastic experience?

Have you ever imagined how Eve must have looked? She was the perfect woman, gorgeous in every way. Physically, spiritually, mentally, emotionally, she was a knockout. I'll bet when Adam saw her he let out a long, low whistle.

Adam was no slouch, either. He must have had the physique of Michelangelo's *David,* the mentality of a genius, and a personality without quirks. In addition, he was spiritual perfection. God created these two perfect creatures and placed within them a positive attitude about sex. If that was the intention of the Creator of the universe, why do His human creations mess up the works?

The Marriage Bed

Many women, particularly those who have been brought up in Christian homes, have negative attitudes toward sex. It is the responsibility of the husband to show his wife that sex within marriage is a beautiful part of God's plan. "Let marriage be held in honor among all, and let the marriage bed be undefiled . . ." (Hebrews 13:4 NAS).

God's positive plan for sex begins with *agape* love. It's the love described in Ephesians 5:25 (NAS): "Husbands, love your wives, just as Christ also loved the church and gave Himself up for her." This is a giving love; in the sexual act, it is giving for the pleasure of the woman, for her enjoyment and fulfillment. Of course, the result will be that the husband will also be fulfilled and satisfied. Love is giving; lust is getting.

In 1 Corinthians 10:24 (NAS) it says: "Let no one seek his own good. . . ." I believe this is the first principle in the marriage relationship. This also applies to the sexual relationship; we should be more interested in pleasing and caring for our wives in the act of lovemaking.

Understanding

In 1 Peter 3:7 it says we are to live in an understanding way. To be understanding, we must be informed; much of this information can be given by your wife, but there are good books on the subject. Listen to her. Some men don't even understand the impact of the menstrual cycle upon the responsiveness and mental attitudes of their wives. In order to reach a state of understanding, there has to be an exposure to the facts.

In becoming an effective narcotic's officer, I spent many hours trying to understand the nature of addicts. What were their thinking patterns, their motivations? It took hours of interviewing, listening to their stories, sitting with them in jail cells, talking in the

alley behind a pool hall. Only then did I begin to understand and
become more able to help them.

I am not implying that women have anything in common with
narcotic addicts; however, the principle of being understanding is
relevant. A wise husband, a fulfilled husband, will listen to his wife
and try to meet her unique needs.

Equals

We are instructed to treat our wives as equals (1 Peter 3:7). For
many men, there is a double standard: Fidelity is a one-way street,
with the wife walking the narrow path, and the husband prowling
through the alleys. The biblical principle is clear: A man and his
wife are partners. In the eyes of God, they are one flesh. God has a
single standard.

I've counseled with many men who are having problems in their
sex lives. They have knowledge of the techniques, have read all of
the sex manuals, and yet are experiencing sexual incompatibility.
Many times the problem is not in the bedroom. The husband-wife
relationship is more than sexual intercourse. Quite often the failure
to adhere to the biblical principle of oneness, being treated as an
equal, is the cause of the problem.

Sexual Prohibitions

When the Bible says, "... let the marriage bed be undefiled
...," it clearly speaks against sex outside of marriage. Leviticus
20:10; Exodus 20:14; and Romans 13:9 all state the extramarital
prohibitions.

Whenever God prohibits an action, it is because He loves us and
doesn't want us to experience pain. During my years in the LAPD, I
have known many men who were "true blue" to their wives, and I
have known those who have played around with one or more
women. The men with their flings may achieve some short-range
pleasure, but they eventually become dissatisfied and disappointed
in this important area of life. Their actions produce the inevitable
pain.

When the Bible says not to covet another man's wife (Exodus

20:17), it is also referring to personal thought patterns. Thinking usually gives rise to action. Contrary to what is being said today, I believe that pornography, sexually explicit magazines, movies, and television are contributing to sexual violence and promiscuity. As a police officer for over twenty-five years (several of those having to do with sex-crime investigation), it is my opinion that pornography does not satisfy sexual desires, but stimulates the observer to act out his fantasies.

Jesus Christ said, "You have heard that it was said, 'You shall not commit adultery'; but I say to you, that every one who looks on a woman to lust for her has committed adultery with her already in his heart" (Matthew 5:27, 28 NAS).

If you don't want to get involved in an adulterous situation, don't entertain the thoughts in your mind! A thousand-mile trip begins with one step.

Several years ago a friend of mine committed adultery. Later he became extremely depressed and was overcome with guilt and remorse. In analyzing how he had come to the point of compromising an earlier pledge and marriage promise he had made to his wife, he explained that it didn't occur with one quick decision, but began with the small steps. It started innocently, just sharing a cup of coffee with this girl. Then there were the luncheons, and, somewhere along the line, thoughts entered his mind. In retrospect, he could see an entire series of decisions that led to the ultimate act of adultery. Taken individually, the earlier decisions did not seem so significant.

I've seen the same progression with the abuse of drugs. I've never talked to a heroin addict who said, "When I was young I decided someday I'd become a heroin addict." No one begins that way. They begin by deciding to associate with those who are taking drugs. Then comes the first hit off a marijuana cigarette. Several decisions later, they find themselves immersed in the subculture of marijuana users. They have already agreed to use a chemical substance to make themselves feel better. A high percentage of individuals who use marijuana will eventually go on to another drug.

The man who doesn't begin the thousand-mile trip by making the first step will have a difficult time getting to an unwanted destination.

Jesus Christ said, "Whoever seeks to keep his life shall lose it, and whoever loses his life shall preserve it alive" (Luke 17:33 NAS). This principle is also true in the area of sexual relationships. An individual who seeks fulfillment at any cost, with disregard for guidance on this subject, ends up losing the fulfillment he desires. On the contrary, the individual who gives up sexual opportunities outside of marriage wins the fulfillment he wants.

Sex Education in the Family

In sex education for our children, I believe we should eliminate negative terms. How much better it is to show disappointment that something so wonderful has been used in the wrong way.

When a boy comes in and tattles on Johnny, we need to be prepared for our reaction and answer. A hasty response might be, "Don't you ever let me catch you doing anything like that!" What has been said to the child in that circumstance is, "You'll probably do what Johnny is doing, but just be careful not to get caught."

Or when we hear that the kids in the playhouse are taking the name of that little shack literally, we might react that, "Johnny is a dirty little boy, and you can't play with him."

Consciously or unconsciously we program our children into negative reactions about sex. If we display Victorian attitudes, without accompanying explanations, we may promote real problems for our children in their marriage relationships. Later in life, they may have trouble giving themselves to their husbands or wives.

When our children are growing up, it is better to display disappointment when someone is misusing this wonderful and powerful act that God has given us. Sex is the consummation of our lives as man and wife. Our sons and daughters deserve to be led into a healthy, positive attitude toward the beauty of sex within marriage. In Christian circles, there are many women who have real problems in the first few years of married life, because they have been told all of their lives that boys are dirty and are just out for what they can get.

I believe that mothers and fathers should do a lot of educating of their daughters before they begin dating. They should not learn that all boys are dirty and nasty, but that we want to utilize the wonderful gift of sex that God has given us, following the principles He has established.

Say Enough to Satisfy Them

Books about sex education make excellent supplementary tools, but there is no substitute for direct communication. A book may be the key to starting the conversation, but sex education should come in small doses, not with the entire bottle of medicine at one time. We don't grab our kid when he's twelve years old and say, "Sit down, I have something to tell you," and then unload everything he's supposed to know. He has probably heard most of what you might say in alley talk, anyhow.

If we come at the subject gradually, as our kids show an interest, we will be able to give them just enough to satisfy them.

The first time my son and I had a talk about sex, he was just a little guy. He was so small that we were playing handball with a volleyball. It was my turn to serve. I dropped the ball and was getting ready to hit it when he said, "How does a baby get out of the mommy's tummy?" Do you know I missed the ball? I thought, *Lord, give me wisdom for what I'm going to say.*

I didn't want to say the stork brings him; he'd know that's a lie. I knew I must have an honest, logical answer for such a pointed question. I told him that God prepares an opening in the mommy's body. He said, "Oh." No more profound questions. He was satisfied and didn't go on at that point.

Many months later he wanted to know how God made that opening. At that time a short answer wasn't enough. I gave him enough information to satisfy him and let it go. None of this, "Let's sit down and discuss it," and then proceeding with sex lectures numbers one through ten.

I remember when we got to the point of talking about fertilization and what the man had to do. He asked, "If the baby is in the mommy, what does the dad have to do with it?" I told him that the daddy starts the baby growing, because he has a seed and gives it to the mommy. He wanted to know more, so I told him that God has prepared a special place for those seeds. Again, he had enough information to satisfy him at the time. Later, when he wanted to know more, I let out enough rope to keep him contented.

With my son, some of the best conversations about sex occurred while we were flying kites. Sometimes the questions he asked were so hairy that I lost track of my kite for a while, but he didn't seem to notice. A lot of parents tell me that their kids never asked about sex. If that's true, there are probably a lot of other things they haven't asked. We began to establish that communication pattern when the children were very young, with the answer-man nights.

As children get the impression that sex is good, when defined and confined in marriage, then they will learn to grasp an understanding of the emotions within their bodies.

Understanding Our Bodies and the Law of Progression

Many young Christians believe that the principles involved in the area of sex do not apply to them. They think, *I'm a Christian, so I'm different.* They think they can get away with certain things, and nothing will happen.

A young couple came to me, disturbed and a little embarrassed. "Mr. Vernon, we're having some problems with sex, and we're coming to you for counseling."

They told me that they thought they were beginning to go too far and were starting to do some things they probably shouldn't do.

I appreciated the fact that they trusted me enough to be open and knew that they needed some advice. I asked them when these things occurred, realizing that they didn't have to be more explicit for me to understand what they were saying. They told me it was when they were parked.

My questions were pretty direct. "Where do you park and at what time of the day or night? How long?" They gave me some obvious answers, since I rarely hear of a young, unmarried couple parking on Wilshire Boulevard during the noon hour.

They said it was usually at night on Mulholland Drive, and maybe they were there two or three hours.

"Do you two understand the cycle of nature?" They looked blank, so I went on to explain. "There are certain laws that operate just like the law of gravity. Would you step off a cliff and not expect to fall, just because you're a Christian?"

The girl was quick to justify their actions. "But, Mr. Vernon, when we park, we begin with a word of prayer."

"Would you step off a cliff with a word of prayer? The law of gravity says you'll go down; the law of nature says there are certain stimuli that shift your whole body into gear. I call this the ice-machine concept."

The Ice Machine and Sex

There's an ice machine at Hume Lake that I find fascinating. When we make homemade ice cream, we go down to the corner and get this crushed ice. We put in three quarters, and, by the time the last coin hits, the ice is on its way, and nothing can stop it. *Zoom*, the whole machine quivers and shakes; I can hear the works inside grinding away. Suddenly, there's the ice. Our bodies are made very much like that ice machine. Even though we are Christians, once those quarters are dropped, look out! When the old ice machine is fired up, it's hard to stop it.

We should be very candid with our Christian young people. There are certain principles that apply to our physical beings and God has given us a mind to understand those principles and not step off cliffs.

The ice-machine concept is the law of progression in action. When we teach our kids to understand their bodies, they should have certain physical reminders of the law of progression.

First, as they are going through puberty, there are aspects of physical change that begin to stimulate the opposite sex. I had a girl tell me that, when she was in junior high, she could remember the first time some guy walked up behind her and said, "Hi," with a new, low voice. She was turned on. This was something she didn't quite understand, but it did something to her.

Progression begins with little things like holding hands. Do you remember the first time someone of the opposite sex held hands with you? However, the next time the hand holding starts where you left off, and from there the arm is around the waist. Next time you go out, you don't start at the beginning, but jump right in where you left off. There may be a little formality of going through the beginning stages, but that's really fast. You get right on with it.

Then there's the kiss. First the little kiss, and, of course, the prolonged kiss, and somewhere along the line, the French kiss. The law of progression says: This is where you left off the last time; that is where you begin the next.

We need to explain to our young people that if you spend a lot of time with the same person, you are getting close to dropping those quarters in the ice machine. The more prolonged and confined the relationship becomes, the closer the couple comes to playing around the edge of the cliff.

This is God-given progression that He designed to get us ready for the ultimate act of expression in sexual intercourse. Kissing and petting are for a purpose, not an end in themselves. I know a lot of young people don't understand this, and they think, *We'll just play around and stop before anything happens.* If we have had open communication with our kids, we should be able to explain to them, by the time they are adolescent, that turning on in the area of petting and French kissing is really preparatory to sex. In my opinion it shouldn't be a pattern for committed Christians. The Bible says to cut out the sex play. It's clearly stated:

> You will remember the instructions we gave you then in the name of the Lord Jesus. God's plan is to make you holy, and that means a clean cut with sexual immorality. Every one of you should learn to control his body, keeping it pure, and treating it with respect, and never allowing it to fall victim to lust as do pagans with no knowledge of God.
>
> 1 Thessalonians 4:2–5 PHILLIPS

Any man or boy who says he can mess around with heavy petting and French kissing and not work up a real passion of lust either has something wrong with him, or he's lying. In the margin of the New American Standard Bible, it defines *sexual immorality* as "the passion of lust." This is clearly talking about sex play outside of marriage.

The standards of the world today are contrary to what we are defining for the Christian. We need to teach our young people, first, to have a healthy attitude toward sex; second, to understand their own bodies; then to know the commands in the Word of God.

Follow the Manufacturer's Instructions

The Bible is very explicit about premarital sex, extramarital sex, homosexuality, and sex within marriage. The Bible is not afraid of words that make our cheeks flush and our collars tight. Both adultery and fornication are forbidden. I don't see that it makes much difference whether you define these terms as pre- or extramarital sex, they are both outside of the will of God.

There are also many places in the Bible in which homosexuality is shown to be against God's orders. Romans 1:26, 27 is a classical example of what God thinks about homosexuality: It says that men abandoned the natural function of the woman and burned in their desire towards one another, also, that women exchanged the natural functions for that which is unnatural.

I can't see how people can call themselves Christians and advocate homosexuality. On the other hand, as Christians, we must love and be concerned for the homosexual, while condemning his or her life-style.

The number-one responsibility for the teaching of sex is in the home. The church and school should be farther down on the priority scale for sex education. The reason I list the school last is because it is very difficult for the school to be involved in areas of morality, and it is dangerous to separate physiological sex from the morality of sex.

It's the same way with guns. It's very hazardous to give someone a loaded gun and tell him to use his own judgment. When the children were young, I had to be extremely cautious about handling my gun around the house. I think it is also risky to have kids who are smart about sex, who know how everything works, and who are told to make up their own minds on how to use it.

In the church we get God's directions, but in the home we should rely on His instructions and principles. You can sex educate your children by beginning at an early age to satisfy their curiosity and give honest answers. We need to ask God for His wisdom, so that we are giving our children enough information that is compatible with their age and ability to absorb.

Who Teaches: Mom or Dad?

Although I think the primary responsibility for education in the home is within the same sex, I do believe it is very important to have that cross contact. With our daughter, Pam, I explained to her when she was dating that I was a teenager once, so I knew what went on inside of boys' minds and bodies. Christian girls, especially, are sometimes pretty naive. They know that something about that bikini does something to a guy, but they don't know quite what it is. If they knew, I don't think they would wear some of them.

I've asked this question in a mixed high-school audience, "Now, guys, I want you to be honest about those little twinkie bikinis that leave everything kind of hanging out. What do they do for you spiritually?"

They usually say, "We'll level with you. It wipes us out—makes our thoughts go off in wrong areas."

These little gals think they can bounce around with every ounce showing, or almost showing, and then not understand why guys paw all over them. I think it's important for a girl to know that a guy can be physically aroused just by sight. When I told my daughter that men are different and that high-school boys only need eyeball contact to have things happen, she was surprised. I reminded her that I had handled this subject a lot in discussions in high schools and also that I didn't have a faulty memory about my own youth. A girl should get this male perspective and be cautioned by her father about her own dress and behavior.

Esther told me that Bob has asked her some questions that only a woman could answer. He wondered, "Mom, what did you think the first time Dad put his arm around you?"

Dialogue between fathers and daughters, mothers and sons, is important, but I think the heavy sex education should be confined to the same sex.

Read the Label

"Thy hands made me and fashioned me; Give me understanding, that I may learn Thy commandments" (Psalms 119:73 NAS).

Lord, you made my body, now give me the sense to heed Your commands. He has made us, and He said that men have certain roles and women have certain roles. It makes sense to use these bodies and personalities in accordance with the Manufacturer's instructions. He gave us sex, and, if He gives us children, we are told to teach them about this wonderful gift.

8

I never thought of a married man as a team builder. A team implies that everyone is working together. A team has goals and objectives. A team is a group of individuals with a common purpose. Considering those definitions, it begins to make sense that a man should build his family members into a team.

Look at that sign over the door, embossed in gold. It says, "FOUNDED IN 1910 BY THE SMITH FAMILY." It exemplifies a family working together, passing on the tradition of a business. It has the sound of solidarity.

Matching sweaters, mother-daughter teas, father-son banquets, putting up the Christmas tree, building a tree house, these are all traditions.

I'm not sure what has happened, but, somewhere along the route of the twentieth century, family togetherness seems to have lost its adhesive power. Individuality has replaced cooperation.

We seem to be stumbling over fragmented families, with each member intent on his own pursuit of happiness. However, basic to our nature, we all like to be a part of a team—as long as it's winning. A small team, dedicated to the same goals, is a powerful force against the juggernaut of disorganized opposition.

Some families believe they are spending quality time together when they are anchored on the couch, viewing prime-time television. I wondered what some of the methods Bob Vernon, the married policeman, uses to bring his family together. I interrogated his son, and he confessed, "We do lots of things together, like painting the house, dirt-bike riding, fixing up the cabin. Sometimes Dad turns off the TV and gets everybody together to play games."

I found it difficult to imagine Chief Bob Vernon sitting down and moving little men on a board, until his son told me the name of one of his favorite games: it's *Clue.* Mystery solved!

C. C.

We Can Do It

One of the most important roles of the married man is building his family into a team. If there are no children, the team may be just the husband and wife. Teamwork is when all members subordinate personal prominence to the efficiency of the whole. That's beautiful.

I'm just fascinated with the way television zooms in on the game of football. When we see instant replay with stop action, we really get a chance to watch eleven men work together as a team. On the other hand, it's ridiculous to see a group of people who are supposed to be working together and are not.

We have a saying in our Metro division that if you break formation during a riot, you might as well keep right on going, because you're going to be transferred out of Metro. The temptation to break formation when you're being pelted with rotten eggs or having urine thrown on you is pretty strong. You've seen it happen on TV, when an officer takes off after someone who goaded him past his boiling point. If that happens in Metro, we say, "Out." We work together as a team. If we don't, we lose our efficiency.

During the Watts riots in 1965 I was at One Hundred Third Street in a fire station. At ten o'clock at night the building was assaulted. About two hundred and fifty or three hundred people were outside, some throwing Molotov cocktails that hit the door of the station. The firemen were gone, trying to put out other fires, while their own house was being burned. A sniper with a twenty-two caliber rifle was taking shots at us through the glass doors. It was getting mighty uncomfortable. There were only about fifteen of us left at the station, since I had deployed the rest of the men to evacuate people who wanted to get out of the area. I said, "Look, if we don't get out and do our thing right now, we're going to lose. They're going to wipe us out. I want you guys in squad formation—now!"

They all lined up in columns of twos. The first four men had shot guns at port arms. "Put your helmets on. When I open this door, run out in double time." We practiced a little bit, inside, before we did it. I stood by the door and said, "Go," and they double-timed it out in pairs, with me bringing up the rear. That crowd of people, some of them armed with rifles and Molotov cocktails, broke and ran when they saw us coming out in this regimented way. The psychology of seeing us organized and working together sent them running so fast to get out of our way, that they left several milk crates full of Molotov cocktails. We just picked them up and took them back to headquarters with us.

I've never forgotten that incident. What tremendous force fifteen organized guys had against two hundred and fifty disorganized people.

How did Communism begin? There were just fifteen or sixteen men who sat down and made a plan to take over the world. They have about two-thirds of the world under the Communist banner now. They were dedicated, with a purpose. Of course, it's not a good cause, but it is an example of what organization and teamwork can do.

The Glue in the Family

In the family, as well as in law enforcement, we recognize that it is very important to have cohesiveness. The word *cohere* means "to become united in principles, relationships, or interests." A family is already united in relationships. We can't do anything about that. To be united in interests may be desirable at times, but not necessarily a top priority. However, to share the same principles is a primary concern. Behavioral psychologists now refer to this as shared values.

Today we don't seem to discuss shared values or shared principles in our families. That goes right back to what we said about communications; we lack the time, or don't take the time, to talk about basic directions in life. It's part of the role of the married man to see that the family is united as a team in basic values and principles.

The team concept is present in what we call body life. The body is not just one type of organ or a grouping of cells and functions; it is a beautiful combination in the same way our family relationships should be. Every member of the body is needed. An ear can't get along by itself, nor can an eye or a nose. Every member of the body is needed and is of value to the other members. It's the same relationship in our family. We shouldn't expect everyone to be the same.

I think the greatest thing a man can do for his son, especially for his firstborn, is to let him know very early in life that he doesn't expect him to be a carbon copy of Dad. A lot of young men get very uptight about trying to follow in Dad's footsteps, especially if the father has been successful. I know the sons of some great men, who are having trouble in life today, because they feel they have to live up to their dads' performances.

The Bible likens family relationships to the body-life concept that we have in Christ. All the gifts that God has given to believers in Him are given to perform different functions. In our families, if we want our children to be exactly like us, that is top ego thinking. God has made each of us unique. It's important to recognize that and to let our kids know.

While growing up, my boy would often say, "Hey, Dad, when you were my age, what did you do?" He wanted to know each and every thing, and I would have to share it. But then I would say, "Wait a minute, Bob, I want you to know that you're not just like me. You have a lot of me in you; you have a lot of your mom in you, too; but you are a unique person. When God made you, He threw the mold away. I don't expect you to be just like me."

Bob is free to be his own man. I want to put a lot of my values into him, because I think most of them are biblical values, but that's different from wanting him to be like me.

In a team relationship, in the body-life concept, there is a union of diverse parts. When one part of the body hurts, the other parts have sympathetic pains. You may reach down with your hand and rub that sore spot on your leg. In a team relationship we care for one another.

Bandages for the Body

The other night I wasn't feeling too hot, but there was a fellow down the street who called and said he had some things he wanted to talk over. I spent about three hours just sitting with him and listening. When he was through, he said, "I really appreciate your caring enough for me to sit up and listen. I know you have a lot to do."

I suppose I received a greater blessing out of that than he did. Caring for one another is important. However, sometimes we take our families for granted and don't extend ourselves for them. After spending an entire evening with my neighbor, I walked into the bedroom after he left, and my wife said, "Do you have some time to listen to me tonight?" Wow, where were my priorities? I said, "Come on, honey, let's talk."

In our body-life relationship, sharing concepts and caring for one another is so important.

When You're Full of Honey

You may say, "You're talking theory, not practice, Vernon. Having your family as a team is a great ideal, but it won't work. You have to motivate people to work in a team."

You're right. Every management executive, every football coach, and every married man must know how to be a motivator. The key is to know what motivates the members of your team. And it's not just sweet talk. Proverbs 27:7 says, "He who is full loathes honey, but to the hungry even what is bitter tastes sweet" (NIV). To a person who is full, even honey is tasteless, but a person who is hungry will eat anything. He wants it. He's motivated to eat.

For some humanistic background, I went to a psychologist called Abraham Maslow. He wrote several books, one of them is *The Theory of Human Motivation*. His premise is, first of all, that man is primarily a wanting creature. He has basic needs or wants which are arranged in a certain order. As lower needs are satisfied, higher needs become more apparent. If the lower needs are not satisfied, the higher needs are not so apparent.

If you look at Maslow's theory as represented by a pyramid, the physiological needs, wanting to fill your stomach when hungry or wear clothing, are at the bottom of that triangle. Once your physiological needs are fulfilled, you begin to get interested in security or safety needs. These would be such things as a house, insurance, and so on. As those needs or wants are fulfilled, then you begin to think about some higher needs like acceptance and love. The next climb leads you to think about your ego needs or self-esteem, the desire for recognition. At the top of the pyramid are self-actualization needs. Even Maslow wasn't sure what those were. After the physiological needs, the safety needs, and the ego needs, there is something else to be fulfilled. I think he was trying to express the need for a relationship with God. He tried to verbalize this self-actualization by saying you were reaching your full potential.

In practice, Maslow is saying that if you have a person who is earning $3000 a month, who has a $150,000 home, a car, nice clothes, and no outstanding bills, it is hard to motivate him by saying that if he works a little harder, you will give him more money. Humanly speaking, it may sound as if he should be motivated by money, but it doesn't seem to work. It doesn't motivate him as much as his need for esteem, acceptance, and love.

I was on a plane with some men from McDonald's. They were in the top echelon of the company and were telling me about an employee incentive they had. One of the men opened his briefcase and handed me some certificates; one was for five dollars, one for ten dollars, and another for twenty. He said, "We drop in on McDonald's franchises and go to the counter to order something. If the person who is waiting on us says all the right things and is generally efficient and polite, we hand him one of these certificates that he can redeem for money. Do you know that over 85 percent never turn them in? They put them in their wallets or frame them, because that recognition was more important than money."

Another behavioral scientist, Douglas McGregor, in his book *The Human Side of Enterprise*, proposed a couple of theories he called his *X* and *Y* theories. Both of these concepts are views on how to motivate people.

The *X* theory says:

Assumption One: The average person has an inherent dislike for work and will avoid it if he can.

Assumption Two: Most people must be coerced, controlled, directed, or threatened with punishment in order to motivate them.

Assumption Three: The average person prefers to be directed and wishes to avoid responsibility. He has little ambition and wants security above everything else.

How many of you who are supervisors or managers feel that way? How many of you feel that way about your children? If you do, you are theory-*X*-type people.

The *Y* theory says:

Assumption One: Expenditures of physical and mental effort are as natural as play or rest.

Assumption Two: Control and threats are not the only way to bring about effort.

Assumption Three: Man will exercise self-direction and self-control in aiming for objectives to which he is committed.

In the last assumption, the most important phrase is "to which he is committed." The commitment to objectives is the function of the rewards associated with our achievement. These are good concepts to consider, but these are theories of man, and we have biblical principles for motivation.

Proverbs 13:19 says: "It is pleasant to see plans develop. That is why fools refuse to give them up even when they are wrong."

The writer of the proverb was talking about being committed to objectives in which we have had some input. When the effort, the goal, or the objectives are those in which you had a part of the action, then you are more committed. Business calls it MBO, or management by objectives. In a family situation, I have a more palatable term.

The Smorgasbord Principle

When my kids were little, they didn't like vegetables. We'd put some spinach on their plates, maybe some beets, and all those things they thought were so bad tasting, and say, "Now just eat a little and you'll learn to like them."

My son was ingenious in using cleverly disguised techniques to beat the system. He had the hide-it-under-the-potato-skin trick. I would look at his plate, and the vegetables were all gone, but when I lifted the potato skin, there they were, carefully camouflaged. Then there was the spread-it-around method. He would take a little pile of spinach and disperse it, so it wouldn't look as if there was much on the plate. If you scraped it into a pile, it was the same amount you dished out in the first place.

However, a strange phenomenon would occur when we'd go to a smorgasbord. When Bob put some of the same hated things on his plate, he would finish them. Isn't that what we all do? Even if you don't like it, it's embarrassing not to eat something you've taken. When Mom or someone else has put it on your plate, there is no ego involved, but when you've chosen it yourself, it's an admission that you goofed if you don't eat it.

In Proverbs it says that it is pleasant to see plans develop, when you've made the plans yourself. If you get halfway through the plan and you find out it's not working, you have to make it work.

Whether members of a team are a factory of people or a family of four, when they feel as though they have had some part in making plans, when they've had a voice in setting objectives, then they're going to be more committed to those objectives.

A family team needs a purpose. Men who are team builders need to know where they are going. If we don't have any goals, we won't have any accomplishments. If they don't have children, or even if they don't plan on having children, a man and his wife need plans, objectives, and purpose. These prevent them from doing things that don't count. We don't have much time here on earth, and it's important to make the best of the time we have. The Bible says, "Teach us to number our days and recognize how few they are; help us to spend them as we should" (Psalms 90:12).

How do we know what is important, what gives meaning to our lives? How do we make those plans and lead our families in objective setting?

Principles of Objective Setting

If there weren't some conditions to examine in seeking God's direction for life, we would all be like tumbleweed, tossed and blown along the road by every gust of wind. Three principles are involved in making plans or objective setting. Proverbs 3:5, 6 provides them. First, trust the Lord with all your heart. Second, don't depend on your own understanding, but follow the instructions in God's Book. Third, in every way, put God first.

At the very beginning of setting objectives, it's important to see God's guidance as the Director of your family. Use God's principles and involve others as participants.

One Saturday I wanted Bob to do some yard work. I said, "Hey, Bob, do you think it's nice to have a neat yard?" He wasn't too sure about his answer, because he knew what was coming next. Reluctantly, he agreed that it's probably a fair idea, because it's not a good Christian witness to have a trashy-looking yard. We walked around the yard together, and I pointed out several things that needed work. "You're on your own, Bob. What do you think you can do today?"

I was having Bob commit himself to an objective. I didn't say, "Now I want you to move that pile of bricks and put it over there, and clean up the shed while you're at it." I asked him what he thought he could do. I was amazed when he said he thought he could wash the windows, clean up the trash, and prune a tree. I think he got up to about number four when I said, "Wait a minute—I don't think you're going to be able to do much more than that by noon. We'll want to take off for the ball game, you know."

Did that kid work that morning! It was the first time I tried this, after thinking about the smorgasbord principle. I wondered why I hadn't done it before. Now the objectives were his plan. I used to give the orders and he would fool around in the backyard, take a drink break every fifteen minutes, and about noon have only a few things done. But when they were his objectives, he really hustled to get everything done.

If the objectives are more difficult to achieve, or it's complex, it's sometimes a good idea to work backwards. I think it's very important with young people to set up a series of subgoals to reach an objective. It's not easy to look too far ahead, when life is being lived for the moment.

The Stair Technique

I asked Bob one day what kind of house he would like to have when he was thirty years old. He described a house, and I said, "That sounds like you're talking about seventy-five thousand dollars." (Inflation will alter these figures considerably.) "What kind of car do you want?" He described the car and a lot of other things he wanted and I said, "Sounds good. Why don't you go out and buy them right now?" I could almost read what he was thinking: *The old man is on to some principle again—guess I'll just play along with him.*

"Dad, you know I don't have that kind of bread. Come on now."

"You mean you need to get the money, right?" Sometimes I can play up to that image of dumb cop without half-trying. "Bob, why don't you get the money?" Bob knew I wasn't talking about anything that's not legit, so he carried on the progression. "I don't have that kind of job, Dad."

"What kind of job would you have to have to live in a seventy-five-thousand-dollar home and have a Corvette and all the other things you want?"

"Oh, I guess I'd have to make somewhere between twenty and thirty thousand a year."

Next step: "Why don't you go out and get that kind of job?"

To his credit, Bob doesn't get exasperated with this type of questioning. After all, we are communicating, and he is contributing. "Dad, I'm not qualified." I kept pressing: "How are you going to get the qualification?"

The answer was slow in coming. "I guess I need to go to college."
"Why don't you go to college tomorrow?"

He said that he needed to get a high-school diploma. On we went. "Why don't you get your diploma tomorrow?" Naturally, he said it's because he hadn't completed the classes or done the homework he needed to do in order to graduate.

We had arrived, climbing one stair at a time, to the point I wanted to make. What I really wanted to talk to Bob about was getting his homework done. We started at the top of the stairs and went down to something he could grasp.

We assume that kids can see this natural progression in why they go to school or do anything. They can't follow it up to the natural conclusion as well as they can trace it down from the objective to the subgoals which are necessary.

One of the greatest football passers the world has ever seen was Johnny Unitas. Do you know how he got there? He said that when he was a kid he hung a tire from a tree and would practice throwing the football through the tire. Sometimes he could get someone to chase the football for him, but most of the time he had to chase it himself. He said, "That wasn't fun throwing a football and missing half the time and then having to chase it. But I never lost sight of my objective. I wanted to be the world's greatest football passer." As long as he kept his eyes on the objective, this step of passing it through the tire took on meaning.

Responsibility of a Team Leader

Are we going to be leaders in our families or drop-outs? If we strive to be successful in anything, and a successful marriage is a great goal, we need to be objective oriented. It's also important to measure accomplishments in relationship to objectives. A lot of bosses, for instance, will set the goals, but they don't let people know how they are doing in relationship to the goals' accomplishment. I think it's a good idea to encourage the accomplishments of your children and your wife as they are working toward an objective. "Hey, son, you're really doing well with that paint job. Watch it around the windows, so you won't have to do a lot of scraping."

Give a little input on the progression of a job, and it shows you are interested.

One of the most neglected areas of traditional American family life is in this area of objective setting. Too many men function in a haphazard way, allowing impulse to determine direction.

We are supposed to live orderly lives that are committed; we accomplish this by allowing members of the family to have a part in goals, by measuring progress, and by rewarding them.

These principles apply in a family, in a business, and in personal living. Goals are not just intended for sports; they are vital in the fulfillment of the true masculine role.

9

The late 1960s were tense in America: Riots and marches increased the national fever over the war in Vietnam. In Los Angeles, students rioted when President Lyndon Johnson visited the city for a major address. Many University of California students were involved in a melee with the Los Angeles Police Department.

With the background of those tension-filled days, Officer Ralph Waddy recalled a summer-camp situation that was sponsored by UCLA and staffed with police officers. Students, between the ages of eighteen and twenty-two, some of them wearing bandages over their riot wounds, were assigned to train the policemen, who were men several years older.

Camp kids had been recommended by the police officers. Some of the youngsters were trained thieves from the slums of the city. One family had children from the ages of eight to fourteen, who were responsible for 25 percent of the burglaries in their district. It was a boy from that family who threw water on Officer Ralph. But that story is in the next chapter.

Camp was trouble from the beginning. The students and the police disagreed over disciplinary measures, and soon conditions deteriorated into mass rebellion. The kids were getting mutinous, throwing rocks, and threatening murder. Officer Waddy had worked with kids for years, but he was thwarted in his attempts to enforce discipline. Finally, Bob Vernon was called to help.

As a result of some hard disciplinary measures, insurrection was avoided. Ralph Waddy told me about Bob Vernon's input into a potentially explosive situation. "Vernon rules by example," Officer

Waddy reported. "Some of these God-squad guys just preach, but not Vernon. He lives what he talks."

Office Waddy described in salty terms the opinion he had of Bob Vernon's ability to switch a negative situation into a positive direction. "Vernon's the kind of guy who can pull it out of the toilet and make it right."

Discipline at that camp produced positive results for years. The boy who was ducked in the dishwater by Officer Waddy became a leading influence in his family, and, as Waddy said, "He straightened his father out." Incidentally, the crime rate in that neighborhood went down.

C. C.

Ouch! I Needed That

Discipline is not an ugly word. However, *punishment* flashes negative signals. I do not believe punishment is the only way to get people to do or not to do something. It's the last-ditch method we use when all else has failed.

The role of the married man is to establish the kind of communication in his home, that leads to understanding the principles of discipline. It is the responsibility of the leader in the home to make sure that the people in the family are communicating with him and with one another.

Discipline and punishment are biblical. They should be used after a lot of time is spent in positive guidance, in love and acceptance. Those are the prerequisites to discipline.

What is discipline? It comes from a Latin word, *disco,* meaning "to learn." (You thought it was "dance," didn't you?) Another definition for *discipline* is "training to act in accordance to rules." In that context, discipline doesn't seem so rough. But it can be!

When I entered the Police Academy, the type of discipline employed there was new to me. I had never been in the army or navy, so I did some funny things. One day we were doing push-ups, and the whole process seemed like a cinch to me. I was in good shape, having been swimming a lot and lifting weights, so push-ups weren't too much of a strain. I was pumping up and down in time, when the instructor came by and said, "Vernon, do it faster."

I looked at the other cadets, and it didn't make sense to me. I was in cadence, so why should I go faster? I said, "I'm going as fast as everyone else." I kept right on with the "Hup, one, two." The instructor got red in the face. "What did you say, Vernon?" Then I made a serious mistake. I repeated the same thing, "I'm going as fast as everyone else."

The guy became excited, and his voice went up an octave. "Okay, Vernon, five laps." I stood up and ran my laps, but the rest of the day he gave me a lot of trouble. Every exercise we did, he would come over and harass me. From then on I did whatever he said, because I didn't want to do five more laps.

When we got into the shower, the guys said, "Hey, Vernon, you've never been in the service, huh?" I said, "No." Then I got the word. They said, "Whenever they tell you to do something, just do it. Sometimes it won't make sense, but do it anyway, okay?"

That's discipline: training to act in accordance with rules. Incidentally, I found out the reason for the Academy discipline. In police work it's essential. Let's say I'm in a building where we have a barricaded suspect. He's firing rounds at us, and the sergeant says, "Vernon, get over there behind that wall." The sergeant knows more about the situation than I do; he has experience, and he's in charge. At this point I don't have time to say, "Let's talk about this, Sarge." Bullets are flying, and I have to do as he says.

Another element of discipline may be defined as "a method of regulating principles and practice." We've all been regulated in some type of principles, either at school or home. Discipline is also referred to as "punishment inflicted by way of correction and training." Normally, we think of discipline in terms of the last definition. It's punishment, right? No, discipline is the total spectrum of training. This is why it's so important to understand it in our homes and to show it through the way we act toward one another, how we treat our kids, and the manner in which we control ourselves.

The word *disciple* comes from the same root: *disco.* When Jesus discipled his followers, he was training them. He didn't go around whipping them, but He was disciplining them. He selected twelve men and spent three years with them. He lived with them, poured His life into them. He inoculated them with His principles for living. At the end of those three years, they were so discipled or disciplined that they went out and spread these principles throughout the world.

As leaders, men need to recognize this concept of discipling followers, whether it be a wife or child or employee. Most important, of course, is the need to discipline ourselves.

Negative Discipline

Punishment is a part of discipline; it is a way of teaching, as long as it is in accordance with biblical principles. Punishment demonstrates love. First, let's look at punishment of children. I know that I'm in dangerous waters here, but I know the principles will justify the actions. Look at Proverbs 3:11: "Young man, do not resent it when God chastens and corrects you, for his punishment is proof of his love. Just as a father punishes a son he delights in to make him better, so the Lord corrects you."

Another excellent proverb about discipline: "If you refuse to discipline your son, it proves you don't love him; for if you love him you will be prompt to punish him" (Proverbs 13:24).

We had a camp situation, some time ago, in which members of the Police Department took some kids from the ghetto area into the mountains for a week at a time. We also had a group of university students who were trained counselors and specialists in camping. Their ideas about the type of program to run for the kids and our ideas were contrary.

We had a regimented pattern built into our program. Everyone got up at 6:30 A.M. and did calisthenics first, then they would march into the dining hall, and someone would yell, "Seats." Everyone would sit down together; it was strict. The college counselors said, "You shouldn't do this. You're forcing people to do things, and we don't think it's right."

One night, in the first week, one black young man was on KP with some other boys. He balked at this job. "Listen, washing dishes is women's work. I'm not going to do it." His counselor, who was a black police officer, said, "You are going to do it." The kid said, "No, I'm not."

The size of the policeman was enough to make the kid decide he should do KP, but he was bitter. His job was to take the dish from the soapy water and put it in the rinse water. As he pulled the dishes out of the rinse, he would give each plate a flip and spray water. Waddy, the police officer, was standing right beside him, to make sure he stayed in the kitchen; consequently, water was getting all over his clothes. After about the third time, it was obvious that the methodical drenching was not an accident, but a pattern, so Waddy said, "One more time and your head goes in the sink."

The kid looked at him, wondering how far he could push, and pulled the next dish out with the water flying. He had to find out if the officer meant what he said. He found out. His head went into the rinse water, and he came up fighting. The officer took the flailing, yelling boy into the woods, and gave him a few whacks on his rear. He brought him back to camp and sat down with him on a log. "Now, look," the cop began, "I can see you're really mad at me, but I want you to think over what just happened. I told you one more time and the head goes in the water, right? You did it one more time. What did I have to do, if I wanted you to grow up to be a man who could really live in this society, where you get a lot of 'noes'? I have to prepare you for that, so you will be a better man."

The kid looked at him, thinking over this whole process. It began to make some sense to him.

Gradually, we saw a change come over this young fellow: By the end of the week this kid, who was such a bitter, antisocial youngster, was following Officer Waddy everywhere he went. Waddy had a cowboy hat, and, every chance he could get, the kid would take it off the officer's head and put it on his own. He idolized Waddy.

At the end of camp, Waddy came up to me with tears in his eyes. I said, "What happened?" He looked down at the ground, hitting his hand with that old Stetson, and said, "The kid wants to come home with me. Furthermore, I want to take him. He said he'd sleep on the back porch, in the cellar—anywhere—if I would be his dad."

The police officer and the ghetto kid demonstrated that the proverb is right. It does demonstrate love to discipline someone and to teach him right from wrong. It shows you really care.

Love Is Not Enough

Dr. James Dobson, a very perceptive psychologist, said in his book *Dare to Discipline:*

Perhaps the greatest and most common shortcoming during the past twenty-five years was related to the belief, particularly by new parents, that "love is enough" in raising children. Apparently they believed that successful parenthood consists of two primary obligations: (1) raise the child in an atmosphere of genuine affection; (2) satisfy his material and physical needs. They expected every good and worthwhile virtue to bubble forth from this spring of loving kindness. . . . Love in the absence of instruction will not produce a child with self-discipline, self-control, and respect for his fellow man.

Life is full of frustration; when someone denies us something because we don't have enough money, that's real life. We have to be disciplined persons to function in our environment. If everything is given to us all our lives, it's hard to live in the real world.

I think the situation in some of our colleges a few years ago was a result of undisciplined upbringing. There were a lot of young people who had never been exposed to denial experiences. They got into school and said, "We want this." The college administration said, "No." Then the students marched into the administration offices and made their demands. They couldn't cope with a no.

Life is full of noes. There are a lot of things that I can't do, that I'd like to do. The well-adjusted person is the one who can learn to cope with the realities of life, including negative answers. Discipline is God's way, and it's for our good.

In the Old Testament there were the sons of Eli, the priest, who were undisciplined; they were ungodly men whose father did not punish them. So the Lord said:

> . . . I am going to do a shocking thing in Israel. I am going to do all the dreadful things I warned Eli about. I have continually threatened him and his entire family with punishment because his sons are blaspheming God, and he doesn't stop them.
>
> 1 Samuel 3:11–13

Proverbs 10:10 says: "Winking at sin leads to sorrow; bold reproof leads to peace." God's way is always the best way; when we don't go His way, we're going to have sorrow in our lives.

Before Discipline, What?

We're talking about negative discipline now, and we need to be convinced that the principles we use are the correct ones. Any adult must get his act together before starting a discipline program. We need to know what we're doing and have some basic principles to follow.

One of the problems I've seen, as a juvenile officer, is homes where parents don't agree. In front of the child, they disagree about discipline. One says, "I think he ought to be spanked." The other says. "That's too harsh. He doesn't deserve that." Finally, when he does get spanked, maybe by the dad, the child begins to wonder if it was fair. After all, his mother thought it was too harsh, didn't she? The child begins to develop a root of bitterness, as the Bible calls it.

One of the most bitter youngsters I've ever seen was antagonistic toward his mother, who was always championing his cause, because he knew deep down inside that he was wrong. He resented his mother for not disciplining him and for being against his dad. He almost hated her.

It's very important to present a united front. There will be normal differences of opinion, but when there is an open confrontation about discipline, it's time to say, "Let's go in the other room." Shut the door and hash it out; when you come out, be in agreement. Then the child will have a sense of security, because you have agreed upon a course of action.

How do we come to an agreement, men and women? We must look to principles and values upon which guidance is based. Proverbs 2:6–9 gives us some insight here:

For the Lord grants wisdom! His every word is a treasure of knowledge and understanding. He grants good sense to the godly—his saints. He is their shield, protecting them and guarding their pathway. He shows how to distinguish right from wrong, how to find the right decision every time.

What a promise! Of course, that promise is based upon knowing His Word, because it says His every word is a treasure of knowledge. This is why it's important to begin, early in our Christian experience, to bathe ourselves in principles from this Book: to memorize them, study them, and read them.

I don't remember every word that I've read, but I'm convinced that reading the Bible regularly is the key to understanding principles. I read a little bit of my Bible every night, regardless of how tired I am. Maybe just six or seven verses will be all I can manage at a time, but I have been fed, nevertheless. How many of us recall what we had for dinner two weeks ago on Tuesday night? Did that food do you any good? Our bodies were nourished and sustained for a time, even though we don't remember what we have eaten. It's that way with spiritual food; we don't remember every single word we've read, but we nourish our spiritual bodies. Second Timothy 3:16 (NAS) says: "All Scripture is inspired by God and profitable for teaching, for reproof, for correction, for training in righteousness."

If we study the Bible we find out what is right and wrong. The word *reproof,* for instance, is strong. An example of reproof is when the funny light shines in your rearview mirror, and the guy with the helmet and goggles comes up to your door and asks, "May I see your driver's license?" Your reaction is very quick. "What have I done wrong?"

"You went through a red light back there."

He has reproved you. The Bible says that Scripture is good for reproof, to let you know right and wrong. Today we desperately need a standard, and this Book will provide the basis upon which to establish your disciplinary program in your home and within yourself.

Now the Bible not only reproves us, but it also shows us how to correct a situation.

Before discipline, the prerequisite is to have some guidelines and then to agree upon the principles. The next essential is to begin with a very important basic assumption; this premise is sometimes hard to compehend when we look at our brand-new, innocent baby, surrounded by soft, pastel blankets, untainted by the pollution of society. Really? Is a child completely innocent?

Born Sinners

Each one of us is born spiritually dead. The Bible says we have all sinned and come short of the glory of God. Consequently, we must expect a child to act in a sinful or rebellious manner.

In our courts and judicial system today, many of the decisions are based upon the fallacious assumption that everyone is born good, or at least neutral, and, as a consequence, anything he does is because something has happened to him. It isn't his fault; the blame should be on mother, father, or society. He is not responsible; society has made him what he is. This basic philosophy has resulted, I believe, in the leniency of the courts today. In one recent year 94 percent of those convicted of crimes in the city of Los Angeles were released on some type of conditional release, rather than doing time in jail. Of those arrested for armed robbery, 44 percent were on parole or probation for a previous robbery count.

The Minnesota Crime Commission made a very perceptive statement. It agrees with the Bible, although it is not a Christian organization. The commission said:

> It must be remembered that no infant is born a finished product. On the contrary, every baby starts life as a little savage. It is equipped, among other things, with organs and muscles over which he has no control. With an urge for self-preservation, with aggressive drives and emotions like anger, and love, over likewise which he has practically no control. He is completely selfish and self-centered. He wants what he wants, when he wants it: his uncle's watch, his bottle, his mother's attention, his playmate's toy. Deny him those wants and he seethes with rage and aggression which would be murderous were he not so helpless.

A baby screams, and his face gets red if he can't have his bottle. If he had more control over his muscles and enough strength to pull the trigger on a gun, if he had one, he would use it.

More from the Minnesota Crime Commission:

> If permitted to continue in the self-centered world of his infancy, given free reign to his impulsive actions to satisfy his wants, every child would grow up a criminal, a thief, killer, rapist. In the process of growing up it is normal for every child to be dirty, to fight, to grab, to steal, to tear things apart, to talk back, to evade. *Every child has to grow out of delinquent behavior.*

What are we being taught today? Many of our institutions of higher learning foster the thinking that we grow *into* delinquent behavior. We begin good and become bad, because of some external pressures or influences. This is wrong. We begin with a sinful nature, and those external pressures make us worse. If you don't have children, just wait; you will not have to teach your children to lie, to be selfish, to punch, or grab. It's a nature we all have.

When my son was a little guy, he had a way of testing me. On Thursday nights when I was watching my favorite program, "Dragnet," he would stand next to the television set, look at me slyly, and reach for the vertical hold. He felt he was the master of the control panel of the world, with all those knobs in front of him. He would reach forward, and I would say, "Bobby, no." He knew what *no* meant, but he'd look at me, turn the knob defiantly, and his attitude would say, *What are you going to do now, big man?* I didn't have to teach him to be rebellious.

Environment has a lot to do with what happens to the individual; it is based upon what is called the onion theory. Like the lowly onion, our personalities are built upon layer after layer of experiences. We are the total products of all those experiences. This is why it's not unusual to have so many murderers today. When you begin with a bad seed and then are exposed to so much violence, such as we see on television, it doesn't shock me that people murder just for the fun of it. It's not right, but it is to be expected.

"A youngster's heart is filled with rebellion, but punishment will drive it out of him" (Proverbs 22:15). When you expect your child to act rebelliously, don't be surprised when he does! One of the biggest problems I have in dealing with parents is that they refuse to accept the fact that their child has done something wrong. I've made a lot of arrests in which I would stop by the house with a young person on the way to juvenile hall. The conversation would go like this:

"Why are you taking my boy to juvenile hall?"

"You see, sir, he's selling marijuana at school."

"*My* son? Absolutely not! He wouldn't do a thing like that."

"Son, would you tell your dad what's happened?"

"The policeman's right, I took. . . ."

"Don't say it! You couldn't do anything like that."

I've had parents tell their kids to be quiet, that the police are making them say things that aren't true.

If we accept the fact that our children are sinners, just like us, and that they are capable of doing almost anything, it will cause us to set up a system to prevent those things from happening. We can help them grow *out* of delinquency. When we accept the basic assumption of a rebellious nature, then we should learn how to establish boundaries and rules to control that rebellion.

Draw the Line Right Here

Two qualities essential for rules of discipline are: They should be clear; they should be consistent.

> And now a word to you parents. Don't keep on scolding and nagging your children, making them angry and resentful. Rather, bring them up with the loving discipline the Lord himself approves, with suggestions and godly advice.
>
> Ephesians 6:4

Loving discipline implies clarity and consistency in the rules. It's not one day it's right to do this, and the next day it's wrong. A child should be able to predict, without asking you, what is going to happen. A child's insecurity and erratic behavior are the results of parents who vacillate over every decision.

We shouldn't have a rule that we can't enforce. I see a lot of parents threaten with things that they know they'll never follow through. The child knows they won't enforce the threat, so he will go ahead and push to see if the rule is really there. One of the biggest problems we all have in the area of discipline is that we don't enforce what we say, either because we're too busy, because it takes too much time, or because some friends arrive, so we let the punishment slip. If your child is really important to you, you will take him into the other room and discipline him as you said you would. "Discipline your son in his early years while there is hope. If you don't you will ruin his life (Proverbs 19:18).

Why discipline? Because we care about our kids. We know that the love and acceptance all of us want in life are built upon the discipline of the Lord.

10

Camp at Hume Lake holds many memories for Tim Savage, but it's not all swimming, football games, or clear mountain air. The lasting impressions on this young man have been the recollections of, first, getting caught for smoking; and, second, throwing a smoke bomb into a cabin. Negative actions produced positive results.

The first discipline resulted in a marathon writing session, in which Tim got a cramped hand, writing five hundred sentences: "I will not smoke." However, the next discipline resulted in injury to another part of his body. And this was humiliating to a seventeen-year-old high-school student, who thought he was far past the age for this type of punishment. Spanking with an oar paddle, at his age? Insulting! "I was furious that I had to receive that treatment," Tim told me.

It all began this way: There were two football teams at camp, and the team Tim was on decided to rout their rivals from their cabin with a smoke bomb. When they were caught in the act, the counselors followed the orders of Bob Vernon in dealing three solid whacks with a sawed-off boat oar. Tim was prepared with padding in a strategic place, but the friend he had persuaded to join him in this prank was not so well protected. His pal limped out after the appropriate punitive measures were taken, with tears in his eyes. Tim, as the mastermind of the prank, was remorseful that his buddy hadn't cushioned the blows, as he had.

"Our attitudes changed after that incident," Tim recalled. "We almost felt honored that the camp leaders took so much trouble to discipline us. But I felt terrible about the guy I had persuaded to join me. I apologized to him for being the instigator. But do you know what? He told me later that it was more than worth it, because that was the week he became a Christian."

And what about Tim? Somehow I got the impression, after talking to him, that those disciplinary measures boosted him in a more lasting way than the initial encounter. For the next seven years, he served as a counselor at a Christian camp and is now a student at Dallas Theological Seminary.

It just proved to me that a rear-end collision could result in a positive forward thrust.

C. C.

Six Steps to
Discipline

"We can't agree to agree." The woman was distraught; her voice quivered on the edge of frustration. "I want to be firmer with our daughter—set the rules and all that—but my husband thinks she needs the freedom to make her own choices. It's a mess. Sometimes I think I'll just walk out on both of them."

Clash—Mom and Dad don't agree; the child is caught in the confusion; and the "peace which passes all understanding" has passed out of the picture. Splattered across America are the broken people who have never known the security of being disciplined in love. Battered children, spoiled adults, and split families are results of freedom without restraints.

I know from biblical principles and practical application that certain disciplinary steps achieve better results than aimless, uncertain action. These methods won't work every time, with every person, because we are treating complex human personalities. However, I know the principles are true; God designed them.

Step One: Cool Off

The purpose is obvious; discipline should be given in love, not in anger. We should be encouraged when we are punished or disciplined! Have you ever heard it said, "This is for your own good"? The Bible said it first, in this way, " ... My son, don't be angry when the Lord punishes you. ... it proves that he loves you" (Hebrews 12:5, 6).

Can we express love when we're angry? Can we be loving when

our tempers are at such a pitch that we are irrational? Children know how to detect the motivation in their punishment; they know whether they are being spanked in rage or in love. There should be a cooling-off period, time enough to allow ourselves to be in control of our emotions. One of the techniques I used was to tell my son to go up to his room. Since we have a two-story house, this would give him time to think over what he had done, and it would give me a breather to simmer down. Whatever technique is used; counting, praying, staring into space, getting a drink of water, they all serve the purpose of taking the heat out of the head.

The battered-child syndrome can be caused partially by a failure to adhere to this first important step in punishment.

Step Two: Explain the Purpose of the Discipline

Cool off first, then make it clear what the violation was. Remember the boy who flipped the water on the officer? He knew what he was doing wrong, no doubt of it. However, a person, child or adult, needs to know that he's not being punished because you are mad at him; you waited to cool off first, so the anger has simmered down. Call attention to the fact that you waited, even when a child is very young.

The purpose of the punishment might be explained this way: "I waited for a few minutes on purpose. I'm not mad at you any longer." (You can hear the sigh of relief, until you say the next line.) "But, I'm going to spank you anyhow, because I think it's right; the Bible tells me to do this. I don't like to spank you, but it's good for your development."

You might use different words, depending on the age of the child, but you explain the purpose of the punishment and your biblical responsibility. When my son was young, I would pull out the Phillips translation of Hebrews 12 and read it to him. Sometimes it's a good idea to explain to your children that you have the authority to set the rules, and to determine what is a violation. In Ephesians 6:1 it says: "Children, obey your parents; this is the right thing to do because God has placed them in authority over you." God is teaching a child through the parents.

Step Three: Knowledge of the Boundaries

It's important for the child to be forced into admitting what he has done. Most of the time he will do this. You should ask, "What did you do? Why is Daddy going to have to spank you?"

"Because I disobeyed you."

"That's not clear enough. What specifically did you do?"

"You told me to be a good boy."

"Okay, but it's more than that. What did I tell you not to do?"

"You told me not to tear leaves from the plants in the backyard."

"Did you?"

"Yes, I did."

A child needs to know how far he can go. When you have set fair rules, he needs to understand the knowledge of the boundaries. Most children, and adults as well, will have a rational explanation for disobedience, but you need to get involved in the admission of guilt.

Step Four: Application

The steps in discipline apply to all types of punishment, but this step is concerned primarily with physical punishment. The Bible indicates that physical punishment should be inflicted with an article other than a hand. "Don't fail to correct your children; discipline won't hurt them! They won't die if you use a stick on them! . . ." (Proverbs 23:13). This is an important principle. It is the reason, for instance, that dog handlers recommend never spanking a dog with your hands. They say, "Love the animal with your hands, spank him with another object, or he'll begin to cower from your hands."

A psychologist friend of mine said, "When a kid is hurt, he gets mad at the article that hurt him. If it's your hand, he transfers that anger to you, and that's not too good."

Even with a cooling-off period, however, the punishment shouldn't be so long after the misdeed that it loses its connection with the offense. It should be soon after the violation. This is not contrary to step one. In Ecclesiastes 8:11 it says, "Because God does not punish sinners instantly, people feel it is safe to do wrong."

One of the elements of any kind of punishment should be some relationship to the offense. This is another reason why our criminal-justice system doesn't work today. It takes an average of nine months to bring a person to trial for a felony offense in Los Angeles. That's too long. In some countries, Turkey, for instance, it is possible to be sentenced and executed within three or four days. Some friends of mine were in Turkey a few years ago when a woman was raped in the hotel where they were staying. The rapist was caught; although they were in the city for only a few days, the man was sent to prison and sentenced before they left. They told me, "They don't have too many rapes in that city."

The application of the punishment should be *soon* after the offense. If Johnny gets a spanking next week for his infraction of the rules today, the punishment will not be effective.

Step Five: Release of Guilt

Unresolved guilt is one of the most destructive emotions. I remember one man whom I met during my police work, whose chin was lacerated with deep scars. The disfigurement was so unusual that I asked him what had happened. He told me that every time he had committed the act for which he had been arrested, he hated himself so much that he went home and slashed his chin with a razor. His offense: child molestation. He released his guilt by inflicting punishment upon himself.

A person, young or old, should have his attention called to his wrongdoing, but know that his guilt has been resolved. Dad, tell your child that you forgive him. God forgives us, therefore we should forgive. A person pays the penalty and starts with a clean slate.

Step Six: I Love You

Children need to be reassured, after punishment, that they are loved. This is probably the most important step. The words are not as important as the action: A hug, rumpling his hair, a wink will speak as loudly as those three little words.

If all these steps are followed, I guarantee it will be effective.

To Spank or Not to Spank: This Is Not the Question

I think physical punishment is necessary at early ages, because it is in the Bible. But what is *early?* It depends upon when a child begins to mature. As a rule, once a child has reached puberty, particularly a girl, I don't think physical punishment is right. I've spanked boys who were as old as sixteen or seventeen. I've hit them with a boat oar, but before you accuse me of extreme cruelty, hear some of the examples.

How does the system of discipline work in action? I am on the board of directors at Hume Lake Christian Camps. We have many young people attending these camps; about four hundred and fifty kids are in high-school camp each week, divided about fifty-fifty between boys and girls. If you don't think that is a problem, you don't know teenagers. Take a bunch of healthy California teenagers and put them for a week in cabins a few feet apart, and you have control problems. Consequently, we have strict rules at Hume Lake. One of the rules is that guys don't go into the girls' area, and girls don't go in the boys' area. We let them know that if they do, they are going to receive physical punishment. Another rule is that they don't use drugs. I say, "Look, if you use drugs, I'm going to spank you with a boat oar."

I have a regular boat oar that I've cut in half. There's four and a half feet of it, which is mostly paddle; it's solid, and I haven't broken one yet.

The first night of camp I saw three guys taking a few hits off a joint. When they saw me coming, one of them ate the rest of it, so I didn't have evidence. I knew what they had done; they knew I knew what they had done. When I came around the corner, they said, "Man, we just got rid of it."

"All three of you been blowing pot, right?"

"Yeah, but you can't bust us."

They knew that without the evidence, I couldn't arrest them. It doesn't take long to become worldly-wise about the law.

"Okay, what did I tell you would happen?"

"You said you'd whack us."

It's a game of wits you play with kids like this. I said, "Look, you're at camp by choice, and you're not my sons. I can't force you to be punished by me. I'm going to give you a choice. Either I will have to send you back home, or I will have to punish you. If you're going to stay here, you have to be under my control. What will it be?"

I haven't had any of them go home after that type of approach. They always want to stay. The next thing we do is phone their folks and tell them what has happened. I say, "I caught your son blowing pot; if you'd like to talk to him and confirm it, that's all right with me, but I'm telling you that I caught him. He's chosen to stay here and submit to my punishment. What do you think?"

Usually the parents say, "How many whacks?" I tell them, "Three," and they frequently tell me to give their kid ten. But I tell the guys, "First offense, I'm going to give you three; that's minimum." The first one hurts, the second one hurts even more, and when the third one lands it's unbelievable. I've never had a kid who doesn't have wet eyes. After it's over, I bring them into my office and sit down to rap for ten or fifteen minutes.

First thing I say, "If I was angry with you, I'm not any more. Do you believe that?" (Step one: cool off.) "Sure," they say, "we can dig it."

Next question is, "What did I catch you doing?"

"We blew some pot." Step two is making clear they understand the violation, so the discipline makes sense.

"What did I say last night?"

"You said if we blew pot, you'd spank us." Step three: know the boundaries.

"I think enough of you guys to follow through. Listen, this is taking time from other things. I could have been playing volleyball, but I'm here with you. I've had to make long-distance phone calls to your folks—big hassle, you know. But do you know why I'm doing this? Because I think enough of you."

Then we go into step four, which is the application. It is a very definitive action. My directions are plain: "You two guys go out of the room. Joe, come here. Take your wallet out of your back pocket and don't put your hands behind your back when I start hitting. I wouldn't want to break a finger." That usually freaks him out a bit. I tell him to bend over and grab his ankles, then I get that boat oar

and give him a good whack. By the time the third one lands, his
eyes are foggy. Then I congratulate him.

"Congratulations. You took it like a man."

Now to step five, which is getting him off a guilt trip. "Joe,
you've paid the penalty, and you're on the same basis as everyone
else in camp. You're not on probation, and I'm not mad at you. I've
wiped the slate clean. Do you understand?"

The kids get a good feeling; if they've had some guilt, it's gone.
Now we come to the last step, which is expressing love. How do
you do that with sixteen-year-old kids who aren't your sons? There
are various ways to express love: You grab the kid by the arm and
sock him in the bicep and say, "Hey, man, I'm with you." Look him
in the eyes and let him know that you care.

Then I pray for him and ask God to help him not to be tempted
again. I've had a lot of boys, with heads bowed, just break down
and sob.

The last night of the camp, some of us were sitting in the lodge
by the fireplace, talking about the victories and problems of that
week. We heard some kids run up on the porch and bang at the
door. The three boys I had spanked were standing there; they were
out of breath and panted, "Is Mr. Vernon here?" The counselor
who answered the door let them in, and they all came running toward me. My first thought was, *My gosh, they're getting even.*
They ran at me and began hugging me. They were all crying. I'll never
forget one black kid who grabbed me, with tears rolling down his
cheeks, and said, "Thank you, Mr. Vernon, nobody ever cared
enough about me before to spank me."

When physical punishment coincides with these steps of discipline, they *are* effective. My wife has kept a file of letters from kids
I've spanked at Hume Lake. Many of them say it was a turning
point in their lives.

At the end of one summer, right after a week at camp, I spoke in
the evening church service at Van Nuys Baptist Church. As I
looked down from the pulpit, I spied six or seven guys who had
taken one of my paddlings during the previous camp session. They
were there with their parents, and I wondered what I was in for
this time. After the service, the parents came up to me and said,

"We don't know what you did to our sons, but, whatever it was, it was fantastic!"

One thing should be clarified. There is a law against child beating, but this is not the same as spanking. Beating is causing a severe injury, and it is an unreasonable act. We are very careful to use a broad paddle and apply it to the gluteus maximus, which are big muscles in a strategic place. It hurts for the moment, but there are no bruises or lacerations. In child beating, there is some kind of corporal injury. The law allows the whipping and correct discipline of a child.

Some parents have said to me, "I couldn't spank my kid; he's too big for it and I couldn't handle him." Many times I've told a mom or dad to bring that child to the station, and I'd supervise the spanking. I hold the kid, while the parent applies the paddle. I have to be careful to keep the parents under control, because some of them get a little hot. It's the first time they've had an opportunity like this, and they really go at it.

I remember one parent who came into the station around eleven o'clock at night. We had picked up his boy, who had been imbibing cheap wine and had become pretty wild. It was a big night at the station, with the hall full of parents and children waiting their turn for counseling. I brought in this parent and said, "Your boy has been tippling a lot of wine. Here's the bottle. Smell his breath and see how he's acting."

The father looked glum. "What do you think I should do, officer?"

I looked at the boy, who was staring at his hands, and said, "I'm not going to file a petition in court, because he's never been arrested before. But I do think he deserves a spanking—and soon." I meant that he should have the punishment when he got home.

The next group came into my office, and in a minute I heard the boy's voice out in the hall, "No, Dad, not here!" I walked outside, and there was the kid, with his trousers dropped, underwear showing, and Dad laying it on him with his belt. I stopped him quickly, "No, sir, not here. Take him home."

I believe these principles will work, even when a child comes from an environment in which he has never been exposed to discipline or punishment. I've seen them work; the letters in my file testify to the fact.

The ideal situation is to begin utilizing these principles right from the very start, in a reasonable manner. When this is done early in life, very little, if any, physical punishment is required once puberty begins. By that time, a strong word, a concerned glance, is all that is necessary.

The principles will work, whether they are utilized early in life or imposed later. It is far better to use these methods early and have a consistency.

When is a person a child, and when is he an adult? Some people are as adult at sixteen as others are at twenty-one. If they are extremely worldly-wise and can no longer be considered adolescents, it is rare that they will respond to any type of discipline.

The manner of discipline I have just described should be used with youngsters who are impressionable. Although we have been describing negative discipline, there is also the positive form. The transition from negative to positive uses the concept of reinforcement. The law of reinforcement aims for behavior which achieves desirable consequences. With that type of definition, I guess I would rather be considered a *law reinforcement officer*. Not a bad title for a cop!

11

We get what we give—and sometimes in a greater degree. A party on one Sunday afternoon didn't happen by accident. It was the result of about twenty-five years of training and five years of planning.

It was Bob and Esther Vernon's twenty-fifth wedding anniversary, which is a landmark in anybody's marriage journey. They had returned from a honeymoon trip to Hawaii, when their daughter, Pam, said that she wanted to have a few relatives in for lunch after church, just to celebrate. Nothing big, you understand, just a cozy little family gathering.

After lunch, the silver-anniversary couple were told to relax and chat with the family, while Pam did the dishes. They talked for a few moments, oblivious to the stealthy tiptoeing from the front door to the living room. Even a cop can be ignorant concerning intruders. But one hundred people! Really, Chief Vernon, where was your emergency beeper?

Pam had invited dozens of old friends, including all of the members of the wedding party, prepared a three-tiered cake, complete with the original bride and groom figures on the top and surprised her parents with the party of the year!

I thought about that party when I saw this proverb quoted in the chapter "You're Great!" The proverb says, "Discipline your son [or daughter] and he [she] will give you happiness and peace of mind" (Proverbs 29:17).

C. C.

You're Great!

Remember Pavlov's dog? A bell is rung every time you feed the dog; soon you ring a bell, and the saliva begins to flow. He's conditioned to know that the bell means food. We can condition youngsters to understand that a certain type of behavior results in things they like.

We're not talking about handing a child a lollipop if he's good; rewards need not be material. One of the most important concepts of a reward is praise. I believe we have so many insecure people today, because they have not had praise in their lives. Praise fosters assurance and confidence.

When a child does something right, pat him on the head and say, "Hey, great job." Even if you have to stretch a little with the compliment, go ahead. Have you ever looked at that little picture he brings home from kindergarten and wondered what it was? Just to say, "That's a neat picture, honey," is good for the child.

Adults need praise, too. I have learned to use this in my management principles with policemen. One day a young sergeant came to me soon after I took over as captain of the accident-investigation division. He said, "I'd like to begin a report-of-the-week club. We're going to put it on the bulletin board." I wasn't sure what this meant, but I let him continue. A harebrained idea is better than no idea at all. The sergeant began to get excited about his idea. "We make about one hundred and fifty traffic reports a day, right?"

The guy was bright, so I figured he had thought this out carefully. He continued, "Why not get the auditor's office to send down two or three reports every Thursday, and you post the one you think is the best investigation of the week."

I thought the idea was off-the-wall. "Wait a minute, Ben. We're working with adults; we're not dealing with a bunch of kids. That's like putting a star next to a guy's name when he's on time or something."

"Captain," Ben said, "can't we try it?"

I gave in, and once a week the reports would come from the auditor's office; I selected the one I thought was the best and circled it with a big red pen. They weren't always spectacular feats; perhaps the officers got themselves dirty by getting under the car to check the brake lining and found out what caused the accident. I might scribble on the report, "Fantastic investigation, went to a lot of trouble—good commitment." I'd initial it and label it REPORT OF THE WEEK.

Two or three weeks after we started this, I walked by the bulletin board about 3:30 P.M. and noticed the early watch, that gets off at 3:15, still standing around. I knew it wasn't payday, so I asked my secretary, "Mary, what's going on? Why is the day watch still hanging around? (The only time they generally stayed later was to get their checks.)

"Captain, you haven't put up the report of the week yet."

I said, "You're kidding me. They're waiting for the report of the week? That Mickey Mouse idea?" I quickly got a report out, circled a couple of things, and wrote, "Good work" on it.

It was important enough for these policemen to get a little recognition of a job well-done that they were willing to stay overtime, without pay, to see who was going to get the commendation. We kept that program going, and, when I went to the Venice Division we started an officer-of-the-month award. We selected an officer whose accomplishments were significant, enlarged a picture of him, and had it presented to him by the local Lion's Club. This was important to these men.

How much more important is recognition to someone who's growing up and needs that security? Attention normally focuses on negative behavior, consequently we have to make a conscious effort to put our attention on good behavior.

As parents, we must constantly force ourselves to watch for positive behavior, give attention, and praise it.

Preparing for Self-discipline

Why do we impose discipline upon a child? We assume that someday he's going to be free and have to make up his own mind about values. He will have to learn how to discipline himself.

The entire disciplinary process in the home should be based upon the assumption that you're preparing your child to be on his own. Someday you're not going to be around to look at him and say, "That's wrong, that's right." We start working toward that day of freedom from the time our children are small. Many parents refuse to accept that concept. They keep the child under their thumbs, so that he becomes dependent upon Mom and Dad for control. When he's eighteen and the control is released, he may freak out and go wild. He thinks, *Now I can do whatever I please,* and begins to do crazy things. The parents haven't prepared the child for freedom.

Men, do you want your children to learn self-discipline? Of course, we all do. The first step in this preparation is to have planned denial experiences. That's what happens in real life, out in the cruel world, where protective parents can't help. When they grow up, people will say, "No, I don't want you to work for me." "No, you can't do that." "No, you can't go there." Your children are going to run into experiences that are against their wills. You have to prepare them for that. If you have the money, resources, or time to say, "Yes" to every question and request, I think it's important to throw in a denial experience, because real life is going to be like that. We must prepare our children for these experiences in the world.

Some people have said to me, "That's hard to swallow. Do you mean if you have the money to let them go to the show, and they want to go on Saturday, that sometimes you say no?"

That's right; if there's no reason to say, "No," then say it, anyhow. This isn't a constant reaction, but a planned denial experience. As an example, my son might say, "Dad, I have all my homework done; I want to watch a movie." I know that he's watched television every night that week, so occasionally I will say, "I don't want any television tonight."

"Why?"

It doesn't make any difference what his age is, every kid asks, "Why?" We must be prepared with answers. "First of all, I'd like to talk. Second, I think it's good to take a breather away from the tube for a while."

A youngster will give objections and react in many different ways. But for him to be able to do anything he wants all the time is a bad pattern. Once he learns to cope with an experience that he knows he can have, but has been denied for some reason, then he will be able to exert self-restraint.

Doling Out Doses of Freedom

The next important concept in learning self-discipline is the gradual expansion of freedom and responsibility. The older he gets, the more freedom you give. This process begins with noncritical issues; you don't want him to mess up his life at a young age by allowing him to have freedom in some important areas. What if a youngster comes to his dad and says, "Dad, I want to smoke pot. What do you think?" And then his dad says, "Well, I'm preparing you for freedom. Make up your own mind."

That may sound ridiculous, but I've actually heard parents say that. Their reasoning, or lack of reasoning, is, "He's going to have to make up his own mind later on, so he might as well learn now."

I believe there are critical areas in which you cannot afford to let a young person make up his mind. However, in the noncritical areas, you can give more and more freedom as he gets older. I do think it's important, even in noncritical issues, to give your opinion about why you would or would not do a particular thing. I tell my son, "I'm getting you ready for freedom." I level with him, let him know what I'm doing. When he was sixteen, I said, "Bob, in a couple of years you're going to be eighteen. I'm getting you ready for freedom, so I'm not going to say you can't do this. However, let me tell you why I wouldn't do it." Then I give him the reasons.

When he was in his late teens, I didn't make my son go to church. Every now and then he would ask, "Dad, do I have to go to church tonight?" My answer was, "Remember what I told you a long time ago? I'm getting you ready for freedom. You don't have to go to church, but let me tell you why I'm going." Pretty soon he would go upstairs, put on his coat, and come down dressed to go. It's great to prepare him for freedom.

Most of the time, a child will do what you want him to do, even though you have given him the ultimate responsibility. When he has had the advantage of knowing your opinion, and you have given him your insights, then he should make up his own mind.

Freedom Plus Responsibility

Many parents give freedom, but they don't accompany it with warnings. It needs to be said, "If you do this, do you know what's going to happen to you? You're going to get hurt."

Freedom also has responsibility. When you tell your child that he can make up his mind on an action, he should know that he is going to be responsible for his decision. I give my son money for working for me, for instance. We painted the house, and I paid him for the work he did. Sometimes he wants to spend his money on things I think are foolish. If he's blowing what he earned, and I don't think it's right, I tell him. However, I let him know that I'm not going to advance money when he sees something else that he wants.

I place the responsibility on him; sometimes it comes back to haunt him. He'll say, "Dad, can I have a couple of bucks?" It's rough to answer, but I'll tell him he blew his money (he knows that), and now he is going to live with the decision he made. The pleas are varied. "But you have plenty of money, Dad. Can't you give me a couple of bucks?"

Placing responsibility on our children is important, but we should make occasional audits on them. Don't take their word for everything they do. The big question will be "Dad, don't you trust me?" I answer, "No." I realize that some people would never say that to their child, but I know how I respond. I tell my child, "I don't trust you, because you're just like I was when I was your age.

It's not you, personally, that I don't trust, it's your adolescence I don't trust. I was there, and when I was your age, I needed some help. I needed my dad to check on me once in a while to keep me where I should be."

A child should know that you *want* to trust him, and this is the reason why you occasionally check on him. If he is doing what he is supposed to be doing, this will build your trust. Sometimes parents trust their children before they are worthy of being trusted. I have walked into pot parties at three in the morning, rounded up a bunch of kids, and called their parents, only to get shocked reactions. They can't believe what they hear. Susie was supposed to be at Linda's house; then we have to tell Susie's astonished parents that Linda was at the party, too. When we call Linda's parents, they say, "She's at Susie's house." They've all promised to be at different places, and they're not anywhere they said they would be.

I think it's important for parents to call other parents and check on overnight plans. It seems basic to me, but a lot of parents don't do it. When I do call, Bob's first reaction is, "Dad, you treat me like a little kid." Then I explain that it's because I care that I want to make sure everything is all right.

Every now and then we have to reevaluate situations when a child has violated our trust. We need to pull back on the reins a bit, until our child proves that we can trust him. Be very candid about this, so that he knows the reasons you have to curtail certain activities, or say no to others.

If you have a teenager and you're not building toward complete freedom, you're going to be in trouble. Hebrews 12:11 (NAS) says, "All discipline for the moment seems not to be joyful, but sorrowful; yet to those who have been trained by it, afterwards it yields the peaceful fruit of righteousness."

The proverb says, "Discipline your son and he will give you happiness and peace of mind" (Proverbs 29:17). Discipline brings the peaceful fruit of righteousness to the one who is disciplined and happiness to the parent. I have heard people say that children can be either the greatest joy in the world or the greatest curse. Some children have gone off on such rebellious kicks that the lives of the parents are ruined; they are in such distress over the children that they can't live happy lives.

To be happy, a parent must have a disciplined personal life and help his child assume responsibility for his own self-discipline. As men who have been given the responsibility by God to assume the role of leader, we need to pray that God will give us the fortitude to abide by the discipline-related concepts we've learned from the Bible.

God may be disciplining us to lead by example. We should make a commitment to spend the time which is necessary with our children, in order to discipline them in love.

Out of self-discipline comes positive behavior. When we say, "You're great," to our wives or our children, they will live up to our belief in them.

12

There's something special about a daughter's love for her dad. My theory is that it can establish a pattern for her view of men or destroy her respect for the masculine mentality.

Pam Vernon Harer is not so far removed from her teen years that she doesn't remember the adolescent disagreements she had with her father. "Sometimes I thought he was too protective. I was very independent and didn't always agree with the rules. There were times when I thought he was too hard on me."

Now Pam has had a few years away from home, enough to make her evaluate her attitudes. "The thing that stands out in my mind was that Dad disciplined in love, not out of rage. His basic concern was for my life. I can't complain now."

It had seemed to me that most of what Bob Vernon had been telling me in this book related to a father's discipline. Knowing, from personal experience, that a mother has the bulk of the disciplinary work, I asked Pam if her mother ever disagreed with her father's strict rules. She didn't need time to think about that. "My folks always seemed to agree; they backed each other. I knew, though, that Mom was my advocate on some issues. She softened Dad, and I'm glad she did."

Pam told me about a time she had lunch with her mom and dad, and fifteen years later remembered what they said. She was ten years old, scheduled to give a piano recital. She said her parents took her to lunch and said, "Pam, you're a good pianist. We're so proud of you." She said that she knew they were in the audience, praying for her, during that recital. "They made me think I could do it. They made me want to live up to their praise."

There was no doubt in Pam's mind that her father was the spiritual leader in their home. Her response to that type of male leadership had its results. Strong spiritual leadership was one of the qualities which attracted her to Steve, her police-officer husband.

It just proves that my theory sometimes works in real life.

C. C.

Delegated By God

A few years ago I picked up a young man for stealing hub caps. I was filling out the booking slip as the boy shuffled in front of my desk. "You come from a pretty good family, according to this address you gave me. What does your father do?"

He told me. I commented that his dad sounded like a responsible citizen and asked him if his father had ever told him it was wrong to steal.

"Sure," he said, "my old man told me."

I knew there was something else on his mind, so I pressed him to continue. The boy said, "My dad steals himself."

Somehow I couldn't imagine a man with a prestige job, living in a good neighborhood, stealing hub caps, and I told his son this.

"Are you kidding? He doesn't steal hub caps, but he steals from his corporation and the government. He makes a couple thousand a year from his income taxes, 'cause he puts in claims I know aren't true. I heard him tell Mom. And he pads his expense account with all sorts of stuff for himself."

It happens too often. The son was not willing to follow his father's words, but rather he followed his example.

The Bible tells us, men, that we are diligently to teach the Word to our children:

> And you shall love the Lord your God with all your heart and with all your soul and with all your might. And these words, which I am commanding you today, shall be on your heart; and *you shall teach them diligently to your sons* and

shall talk of them when you sit in your house and when you walk by the way and when you lie down and when you rise up.

Deuteronomy 6:5–7 NAS, italics mine

We're commanded to do this! Not many men in America know this, do they? They leave the kids to Mom, the school system, or a well-meaning friend or relative. But teaching our kids and sharing with our wives the benefits of biblical principles will surpass the advantages of a new car or a mink coat.

In Psalm 119, the longest chapter in the Bible, there are listed many results of Bible-study teaching. Psalms 119:9–11 speaks about keeping the Word of God so that " . . . I may not sin against Thee" (v.11 NAS). One of the reasons we are to teach our children is to help them cope with sin. This psalm also says that the testimonies of God are "my counselors"; strength and wisdom will come from the teaching of God's Word. We find help when we are in trouble: "Remember the word to Thy servant, In which Thou hast made me hope. This is my comfort in my affliction . . . " (Psalms 119:49, 50 NAS).

These are many of the reasons we are to teach the principles from the Word to our children: to help them cope with sin, for good advice and counsel, for wisdom, for help in trouble.

The Family Priest

Priest is a word which comes from the Greek, *presbyteros,* from which we get our word *presbyterian.* It means "elder," or one authorized to represent, or act as a mediator, of God. In God's line of authority, we know that Christ is the head, and under Him comes the man. The man is to be the representative of God, Jesus Christ, in the divine order of relationships.

In the Book of Job, the oldest book in the Bible, we find out that Job would rise up early in the morning and offer burnt offerings for his sons and daughters; he would consecrate or sanctify them. Job acted as priest for his family. He cared enough about his children that his concern for their spiritual cleansing was uppermost in his mind.

Since we need to *give* spiritual direction, the obvious assumption is that we must *understand* the Gospel ourselves. To find the essentials of the Gospel, read 1 Corinthians 15.

The details of this Gospel begin with the understanding that God has a plan for each life. I think our children should know, as they are growing up, that God Almighty, Creator of the universe, has something in mind for them. He has a plan for joy on earth: " . . . I came that they might have life, and might have it abundantly" (John 10:10 NAS). He has a plan for the future: " 'For I know the plans that I have for you,' declares the Lord, 'plans for welfare and not for calamity to give you a future and a hope' " (Jeremiah 29:11 NAS).

God may have these plans for us, but man has separated himself from God, because of sin. That may not be an acceptable idea to some, but we need to understand that we sin because we are sinners; we are not sinners because we sin. All children have to grow out of delinquency. In the same way, we are born delinquents, or born sinners.

Jesus Christ is God's only provision for man's sin. The Bible says: "And there is salvation in no one else; for there is no other name under heaven that has been given among men, by which we must be saved" (Acts 4:12 NAS). In other words, there is no way we can pull ourselves up by our bootstraps.

Some men may be thinking, *You mean, as a father, I should go over this heavy doctrine stuff with my kids?* We are the family priests, and this is the responsibility God has given us. If we are responsible for the physical well-being of our children, how much more responsible are we for their spiritual well-being?

I remember going over with my son, the basics of what it really means to be a Christian. I did it several times when he was a little guy, and I wasn't sure he was understanding. One day we were out in my mother's garage, getting ready to paint her house. He was pretty excited about the project, so I was letting him help me mix paint. He was seven years old and having a great time adding the tint, then a little thinner, and mixing it with a paddle. He was stirring away, looking down in the bucket, when he said, "I've never asked Jesus Christ to come into my heart."

I was stirring, too, and I thought, *Wait a minute, did I say something about God while I was mixing paint?* I must have been speechless, for once, and he repeated what he said. (Dads can be so dense!) "Can I do that here in Grandma's garage?"

Right there, with the paint fumes in my nose, my son invited Christ into his life. It was a fantastic experience; I'll never forget it.

From Belief to Commitment

The fact that Christ died is known in history. Many people know the facts, but not the reason. One evening we were finishing up a seminar, when one of my associates asked me a leading question. "Bob, Jesus Christ died on a cross, didn't He?" This was a tough cop talking, a guy who had lived through some rugged situations. He was genuinely perplexed about the death of Jesus. "I just began to study what He went through on that cross—physically, I mean. Bob, why did He go through that drill?"

Here was a cop, knowing firsthand about pain and death and wondering why Christ died. I told him about Romans 5:8. It says, "But God demonstrates His own love toward us, in that while we were yet sinners, Christ died for us" (NAS). That, I told my friend, is why He "went through that drill." God showed His ultimate expression of love by giving His only Son to die for our sins. We reestablish contact with God through Christ—and *only* through Him.

Believing that Christ died for us and bringing our belief to the point of commitment are two different things. Many people think they are Christians, but they're not. They believe, but they have never done anything about it.

The best way I can explain belief and commitment is with bulletproof vests. These are an important part of a policeman's equipment. They weigh about four pounds and are about one-fourth of an inch thick. The layers upon layers of special nylonlike material make them awkward and hot to wear. Not many cops are interested in them until something happens to make them take notice.

Last summer, during the middle of August, I received a phone call about 10:30 P.M. It was a hot, sultry summer night; I know when the phone rings that late it's probably my office. It was. The lieutenant from IHD (Investigative Headquarters Division) told me that two of my men had been involved in a shooting. One of them had been hit in the chest and had been taken to the California Hospital.

I threw on some clothes, jumped in my car, and rushed off to the scene, listening to the police radio for further developments. On the way I stopped by the command post and checked with the watch commander. He had a perimeter set up around the area and was beginning a door-to-door search, hoping to find the suspects who had been involved in the shooting. The information at this point was sketchy, and since the investigation at the scene appeared under control, I hurried to the hospital.

As I walked into the emergency room, to my amazement, I saw the wounded officer, Pearson, sitting up in a bed, talking with the doctors and nurses. Pearson's partner, in uniform, was standing beside the bed, and when he saw me come in he began telling me what happened. I couldn't understand why they were both grinning.

They had stopped their patrol car to investigate a group of men loitering in a dark alley behind a hotel. They separated and went around opposite sides of the building. As Pearson got about twenty yards away from them, one of the group opened fire. The first bullet struck him dead center in the chest, knocking him to the pavement. A second round grazed his arm as he fell.

Pearson's partner reached him just as the assailants ran off into the night. He dropped to his side and put out an officer-needs-help call, requesting an ambulance. As he examined Pearson, he was horrified to see a bullet hole squarely in the center of the officer's uniform shirt. Pearson appeared gravely wounded. When asked how badly he was hurt, he responded, "I'm hit bad. I may not make it."

His partner told me, "I thought he was dying. Then I noticed there was no blood oozing from the hole. I pulled his shirt off and saw he had on his bulletproof vest. With my flashlight I located the bullet, still protruding from the vest. It hadn't penetrated."

I said to him, "Pearson—you're wearing your vest, man! You're going to be all right!"

Pearson had to remain in the hospital several days to recover from internal injuries caused by the impact of the bullet, but the vest had saved his life.

A few months before this book was written, another young officer faced deadly gunfire. He was working a one-man report unit, called a U-boat by Los Angeles officers, because of its radio designation *U* before its district number. His primary responsibility was to respond to crime scenes after the fact, to document an investigation. *U* units are not expected to perform aggressive police work.

Late in the evening, an all-units call was broadcast, describing an armed robbery suspect and the vehicle he used to flee the scene. The young officer spotted the car moments after the radio alert. He began following the auto, but wisely chose not to attempt a "pull over," but requested an emergency backup. Since he was in a marked police car, the bandit apparently noticed him following and took off. A high-speed pursuit resulted, with the bandit finally losing control and crashing into an auto-parts store. The criminal's car was severely damaged. The police officer approached the crashed vehicle, probably with the intent of rendering aid to the criminal. At this point he ignored normal officer-safety procedures, due to the severity of the damage. He was met by a hail of gunfire and was struck in the chest. He died within an hour. Investigators at the scene found the young officer's vest on the front seat of his patrol car.

Officer Pearson believed in the importance of a bulletproof vest. He took that belief to the point of commitment, by wearing it, whether it was comfortable or not.

The Bible says, "But as many as received Him, to them He gave the right to become children of God, even to those who believe in His name (John 1:12 NAS).

Belief must be put into action. Action is putting the money on the counter, purchasing the vest, and wearing it.

I think it's up to us, men, to know the difference between simple belief and an active step of faith; then it is our masculine role to let our children and our wives know what the Gospel means and point them toward commitment with the bulletproof vest.

From Commitment to Life-style

Is there anything different about a Christian? Does his life-style reflect his commitment or condemn him as a hypocrite? In the first century, after Paul and the disciples had proclaimed the Gospel in

Asia, the Christian life was referred to as the Way. These Christians were different, their manner of living was based upon different standards, and this was disturbing to many people.

Historically, the first-century Christians were living in a society much like ours. Immorality, perversion, and shady business tactics were prevalent then, just as they are in modern America. When these early Christians began to change some of their living habits, when they stopped visiting the temple prostitutes and indulging in loose living, other people started calling them followers of the Way, which was a distinctive new way of life.

The responsibility of the family priest is to make sure his family understands the Way: the Christian life-style. Being a Christian is more than being a good person. The life-style is secondary to the belief, decision, and commitment. It is the result, not the cause. The Scriptures give us the principles; as the family priests, we need to study them.

"All Scripture is inspired by God and profitable for teaching, for reproof, for correction, for training in righteousness (2 Timothy 3:16 NAS).

Teaching is the step one that we have covered. It is our responsibility to teach the plan of salvation to our families. *Reproof* involves the knowledge necessary to distinguish between right and wrong behavior. *Correction* means to correct the situation, once something has been done wrong. *Training* is needed to prepare for the tests of life.

Training for the Tests

Police training is rugged. Some men who have been through marine boot camp have said that the Los Angeles Police Department training is tougher than the marines. A lot of the men who go through the Academy wonder why we do things the way we do. For instance, we do a lot of running. The first few weeks, the men run a mile and quarter, but by the time they finish they make a six-mile run, and that's not on flat ground. At the end of a long run, there's a hill; and, by the time you've gone six miles, you know the challenge of that hill. It takes training, stamina, and determination to make it to the top without breaking stride.

Training is not just for physical stamina, but also for the proper mental attitude to enable you to go beyond what you think you can do. Training is the foundation for the tests of life. The Bible is the weapon we use in the spiritual warfare of life, in the spiritual tests which confront us.

Eye Test

I was attending a seminar at Northwestern University, playing handball to keep in shape, when my right eye became the target for a very hard handball. I was knocked to the ground, and when I came to, all I could see were some funny gray webs and then nothing. The next few days were dismal; the doctors thought I was going to lose the sight in my eye, or at least have a detached retina. The fellow policeman who hit the ball was in low spirits when he came to see me. I consoled him, "I believe that God allows everything that happens to me for a reason. It may finish my career as a law-enforcement officer, but if it does, He has something better in mind."

There were about fifty men, from all over the states and some foreign countries, at the college. By the end of the semester, I had the opportunity to share Christ with the entire class, because of that injury. It wasn't an accident. God had prepared me for this weeks before, when I had studied the Book of Job.

When I was being wheeled through those hospital corridors on the gurney, the thoughts raced through my mind that I was through as a law-enforcement officer. Being a cop was a life-long ambition; inside my pounding head, I was questioning God. *Why have You done this to me, God?* Then I remembered Job.

"Though he slay me, yet will I trust in him . . ." (Job 13:15 KJV). Here I was, ready to give up my future because of one eye. I felt pretty small and told the Lord I was sorry for my lack of faith. I remembered how God had blessed old Job, because he just hung in there. The Lord gave me the strength I needed for that test.

Every day of our lives we are in training for life's tests. As husbands and fathers, we will be fulfilling the role God intended for us, the role He delegated to us: to be the spiritual leaders in our homes. We don't have to wear a turned-around collar or a pious expression to be the family priest.

13

I've often wondered about men and women who are civilized in every way, but practice mental voodoo upon each other. One takes a jab at the other with a look, a criticism, or a sarcastic laugh. The other grabs the pin and sharpens it for the return thrust. They become wounded, but not fatally—just enough to cause injuries that never seem to heal.

There used to be an old ballad which said, "You only hurt the one you love." Why is that? Is it masochism surfacing, wanting to hurt so that we will be hurt in return?

Of all the principles in *The Married Man*, the one in this little chapter touched me the most. I wonder if this is the reason we see all of those entwined hearts on car windows, which announce that the occupants have attended a Marriage Encounter.

Bob Vernon's suggestions concerning healing family relationships could be the best medical advice given in America. When a person learns those powerful three little words, the wounded patients may experience a fast recovery. Prescription is: *I was wrong*.

C. C.

When There's Pain

A boy was studying anthropology in school and was interested in customs of different countries. He was reporting some of his discoveries to his father. "Do you know, Dad, that in some parts of Africa, a man doesn't know his wife until he marries her?"

His dad was unimpressed. "Why single out Africa?"

Marriage is a continuous education. To stay at the top of the class, it requires constant study. Many married couples have great relationships. But it can be better, much better. Below the surface of wedded bliss, there may be problems which are seething. Bitterness toward each other may be festering quietly; memories of past hurts may be lingering.

Some husbands who have been reading this book might be thinking, "Vernon, if you knew what I know about my wife, you couldn't love her." Or some wives may be saying, "If you understood my husband, you wouldn't talk to me about submission. There's something that happened five years ago that I'll never forget."

Resentful memories and past injuries can cause such pain that barriers are built between husband and wife. There is a principle of healing that God has given us, for He knows our human nature and the hurts we harbor: "Therefore, confess your sins to one another, and pray for one another, so that you may be healed . . ." (James 5:16 NAS).

Do you want your relationship to be healed? Do you want to begin with a clean slate, with the ease of an open relationship? The biblical principle of healing begins by confessing your sins to each other.

Several years ago Esther and I took Pam, who was in high school at the time, with us to a Bill Gothard seminar. Sitting there, listening to some biblical principles, I was convicted of something which was bothering me in my own family life.

For about a year, I had realized that there was a barrier between Pam and me. We didn't have the easy give-and-take that we used to have, and it bothered me to sense this strained relationship.

I heard this principle of confessing your sins to one another and admitting when you're wrong. When we got home, while it was still fresh in my mind, I went into the dining room, put a pad of paper on the table and said, "Pam, I want you to put down some things that have bothered you about me for the last few years. Just list anything that you remember where I was wrong."

"Oh, Dad, I couldn't do that."

"Maybe there are things you're holding against me; I just want you to put down something."

Pam wasn't an immature child; she was a young lady who would soon leave for college. Reluctantly at first, she began to write.

I started to write myself. "I'm going to do the same thing, Pam. I'm going to list some things you've been doing the last couple of years that have bothered me."

Pam made a list, but one item was rather predominant. She had written that about a year and half prior to this time, she had come home fifteen minutes late. I had told her to get in at 11:00 P.M., and she came in at 11:15.

I could remember the incident vividly. I had stewed and seethed during those fifteen minutes. I had judged her guilty before she walked in the door. As far as I was concerned, I had passed sentence on her before she had a chance. When she came in the door, I raised my voice and shouted, "You're grounded for the next two weeks! You can't go anywhere, except school."

Pam was a cheerleader at the time, and the team had a game coming up in a few days. Her eyes began to mist over. "You mean I can't go to the game? Daddy, that's unfair. You're punishing the whole cheerleading team. I have to be there; I'm part of the routine."

I was unwavering. "You can't go."

About a half hour later, I knew I was wrong; I realized I had been too severe, but my pride wouldn't let me back down. I remember listening to Pam sob upstairs in her bed that night. In spite of the sick feeling I had in the pit of my stomach, I stubbornly held my ground.

That incident was still in her mind a year and a half later, as we sat in the dining room. I looked at what she had written, and turned to the daughter I loved so much, and confessed, "Pam, I know I was wrong. I knew fifteen minutes after I said it, that I was wrong. Will you forgive me for doing that to you?"

Tears began to flow down her cheeks, and my face was pretty wet, too. We just grabbed each other and had a good cry. She choked, "Of course I forgive you, Daddy."

Healing took place in our relationship. Some people might believe that a parent shouldn't admit to a child that they're wrong. It lowers the image. I believe it works in the opposite way. Pam knew I was wrong—that wasn't news to her; however, by my admitting to her that I was wrong, I went up a few notches in her book.

It worked both ways. Pam also asked me to forgive her for being bitter about that occasion. She was relieved of that bitterness. Our relationship was back to the way it used to be, after a year and a half of grating on each other and knowing that something wasn't quite right. When we asked each other for forgiveness, it brought that growth that was sapping our relationship to the surface, lanced it, and spewed out all the poison.

Bind the Wounds

If there are things you have been holding inside, bring them out and open the opportunity for those healing words, "Honey, will you forgive me for that?" However, this requires give-and-take on both sides. Both of you must be willing to say, "I was wrong."

The Bible says to "confess your sins to one another," not to the whole world. I don't think we should stand up in a testimony session and say, "Five years ago I had an unclean thought about my wife's girl friend. I wanted to go to bed with her. I want to confess this to everyone." Leave that unsaid. The only one who knows about that is God, and you confess that to Him.

However, if your wife knows about something, you should confess to her. Likewise, husbands, make your wife aware of what is bothering you. If you've been carrying a grudge or you're bitter, it's sapping your love for each other.

Women, if you are convicted that your attitude toward your husband has been one of dominance, not submission, you need to tell him, "I have been trying to get control, to henpeck you. Will you forgive me for that? I know it's not God's way."

Men, some of you need to tell your wives, "Forgive me for not loving you in a sacrificial way. Forgive me for thinking more of my wants and desires than yours. By God's grace, I want to love you as I should."

I know this is against our culture. Everything within us tells us to remember every insult, every broken promise. But God's way is one of confession and healing. With His principles, the marital relationship will be restored and become better than it ever was—*much better.*

Complete Healing

There's a postscript to my story about Pam and the healing power of confession. Seven years after our father-daughter session at the dining-room table, I was speaking for a conference of police officers and their wives. Pam and her husband were in the audience. I didn't want to embarrass her, but I told the story I have related in this chapter.

After my talk was over, she came up to me and said, "You know, Dad, my resentments and attitudes were so completely healed that I had even forgotten the incident."

The cure was complete.

14

Have you ever noticed how married couples begin to look alike after many years? It's not that facial features change, but it's an inward transition.

A bride is always lovely; she has the anticipation of an unknown life with a man she thinks she knows.

A young married is uncertain, having charted some of the course and found herself perplexed by some of the detours and roadblocks she hadn't seen on the wedding map.

A young mother is harassed, beginning to appreciate what her own mother went through, and not being able to see the end of the work and fatigue.

But when a woman's children are grown, when the dinner table is set for two and the earlier distractions and interruptions of family life have eased, the face of a marriage is clearly reflected.

I know that Chief Vernon is qualified to write this last chapter. You see, I know Esther Vernon.

C. C.

How to Have a
Beautiful Wife

The transition from street police work to the role of manager was difficult for me. On the street, you don't have to look at the big picture; you respond to calls for service, catch the bad guys, and help people in trouble. It was actually fun. However, when I became a manager, I had to start thinking in terms of goals and ways of measuring effectiveness. Now it was my job to give direction to the street cops. I had to analyze a total situation, to figure out where we should be heading as a team and how to get there.

Policemen are just like everyone else. We would rather do the easy jobs first and shy away from the difficult tasks.

For several years I was captain of the Venice Division of the LAPD. Venice was an interesting assignment. The area included the International Airport, Dockweiler State Beach, and the infamous Ocean Front Walk, where it seems all of the runaways in the world land. I noticed that when my men had any free time between calls, most of them would gravitate to two or three locations in the division, known as "hot spots." These were the locations where most of the hoods hung out. It was easy to make an arrest, especially for narcotics or weapons violations.

The officers were oriented toward making arrests, chasing crooks. Whenever they had a chance, they would slip by one of the hot spots, even if it meant leaving their own patrol districts, and arrest someone holding dope or packing a gun. If you asked any cop at that time who the good cops in the division were, they would give you a ready list. They all had one thing in common: lots of arrests, good arrests, not "hummers" (close-call types). In other words, the good guys were high producers as far as traditional police work. But, in spite of the arrest record, the biggest crime problem in Venice—burglaries—continued to rise.

I wanted to be more effective against the burglary problem, so I took one-sixth of the personnel resources of the division and assigned them about one-sixth of an area, with a lieutenant in charge. This was called Team 28, and their designated area had the biggest burglary problem. I told them I was not interested in the number of arrests they would make; I was only interested in reducing crime, particularly burglaries. I explained that I didn't care how they did it, as long as their actions were legal and ethical. Results, not production, were important.

It was a tough transition. The organization was changed, but more important, the role expectation was altered. Police officers began to be evaluated on the basis of crime reduction, rather than arrest production. The true test of the effectiveness of the police team was the absence of crime in their district.

The results were astounding during that first year. The concerned officers changed their own roles in the community. They began spending more time on crime-prevention efforts, organizing the communities into neighborhood watches with over two hundred block captains. They still made arrests and caught the bad guys, but now they were accomplishing much more. Crime went down over 20 percent during the first year.

It was all the matter of role definition. In the first instance, they envisioned themselves as arrest makers. In the second instance, which is a more accurate role, they perceived themselves as crime reducers. This different method of evaluating their effectiveness— the absence of crime in their area—caused them to change their performance.

Cops and Wife Robbers

I think a similar situation exists with many men in our society. They're working hard at being husbands and fathers, but they have an inaccurate role perception. Many of us believe that success as a husband is measured in terms of the price of a house, the size of a car, annual income, status in the community, and the number of service clubs we join. I wonder how many men would use a man's wife as the criterion for measuring effectiveness as a husband. Do you know that the Bible lists just that as a means of evaluating a man?

The Bible states in 1 Corinthians 11:7 (NAS): ". . . the woman is the glory of man." We don't use that word *glory* very much any more, but the dictionary states that it means "something that brings praise and honor, source of pride and joy." In other words, a powerful way of evaluating a man's effectiveness as a husband, or the way to determine if he should receive honor and praise as husband, is to look at his wife. What type of woman is she? Has she reached her full potential? Is she beautiful in every sense of the word? This is the biblical way to evaluate whether or not a man is doing his job as a husband: Look at his wife.

A man may have a good job, high position, attain wealth and personal fame; but, according to the Creator's principle, he has failed if his wife is a failure. A so-called successful man whose wife is a total wreck, alcoholic, or psychotic, is perhaps not so successful after all.

The biblical principle is that two shall become one. If a wife is unfulfilled, undeveloped, lacking in direction and purpose, in a real sense all of these failures accrue to the husband, since they are really one in God's sight. A sickness in any part of this couple reflects on the unity of whole.

I'm sure you've been at a reunion where people are meeting friends they haven't seen for many years. When someone meets a woman who has grown in beauty over the lapse of time, the comment is often made, "Your husband must be treating you well." Many times this is said in jest, but how true it is! Little do they know they are agreeing with the principle that is centuries old and originates from God Himself.

There is a parallel between many of us, as husbands, and the officers of the Venice Division. Those policemen, while making record arrests, were involved in legitimate efforts, but they were not really addressing the major issue. Men, do you have beautiful wives? Do you want more beautiful wives? This is the issue.

It's an Act of the Will

First of all, you love your wife in the real biblical sense. We've discussed the meaning of the word *agape*, and this is the first principle I would like to develop further. *Agape* love is giving love. This is the primary and foundational commandment given to husbands in reference to their wives. It's so simple and yet so profound. "Husbands, love your wives . . ." (Ephesians 5:25 NAS).

I've talked with some men who say, "I can't be commanded to do something I don't have the capacity to do." They state emphatically, "I can't will to feel something that's not there." Some others say, "I wish I could love my wife, but I just don't."

What they are all really saying is that they don't have an erotic or passionate attraction to their wives. However, I believe they are confusing a personal feeling with an act of the will. That command to love our wives is not a command to have an emotional sentiment over which we have no control. It is a command to give of ourselves to our wives, whether or not we have the emotional attraction. The incredible part is, when we begin to obey and give in every respect to our wives, the emotional or erotic attraction will follow.

I'm an avid jogger. I jog almost every morning of the week, a minimum of five days a week. I have recently worked up to five miles at a time. When I began jogging, I felt terrible. My body wasn't ready for it. I had to progress slowly; first of all, jogging just a few hundred yards and then walking until I could get my breath back. Eventually, I broke through the one-mile barrier and then the two-mile barrier. Although I've run for several years, I still feel uncomfortable when I first begin. However, somewhere around one mile, I break through and become elated, almost euphoric. After the run, I feel better all day. My general physical condition and well-being is better today than it was when I was in my late twenties and out of shape. When I relate my jogging experience to some of my friends, I often hear the phrase, "If only I felt better, I would run, too." The point is, they won't begin feeling better until they do run. It's something you just have to start doing. It's an act of the will. After you exercise that act of the will, you begin to feel better physically.

I think there is a parallel between the *agape*-love and emotional-love relationships and physical conditioning. You must *will* to act the first kind of love in order to achieve the second. But the second doesn't come unless you do the first.

God would never command you to do something you do not have the capacity to perform. He commands you to love your wife in a giving way. You can do that. I believe the reward will be that you will be drawn to her physically, emotionally, and spiritually, when you obey that command.

Love Has Many Meanings

A list of instructions came with the love process. It's exciting to see how well these Manufacturer's directions work: "Husbands, love your wives, just as Christ also loved the church and gave Himself up for her; that He might *sanctify* her, having cleansed her by the washing of water with the word" (Ephesians 5:25, 26 NAS, *italics mine*). The word *sanctify* is not a word we use in normal conversation, but it means "to clean, to keep pure." A man who really loves his wife will try to *protect her* from corrupting influences.

In my line of work, I've seen some opposite attitudes: husbands who have sent their wives out on the street to sell their bodies. These married prostitutes are mistakenly bribed in the name of "love." Their husbands will say, "If you really love me, you'll do this for me."

Real love is interested in the safety and protection of the loved one. In California, we have a law prohibiting conduct which is termed "disturbing the peace." In Section 415 of our penal code, it describes certain acts which are prohibited: "the use of any vulgar, profane, or indecent language within the presence of women or children." There is a law similar to this in virtually every state of the union. Society recognizes that it is proper and just to protect women from certain corrupting influences.

I used to wonder why the law requires a higher level of conduct in the presence of women and children. However, since the biblical principle in Ephesians instructs husbands to protect their wives that they might be "holy and blameless" (Ephesians 5:27 NAS), I began to examine the practicality of it. It's the nature of the pragmatic policeman in me.

At one time, I was sent to a special captain's school, conducted by the industrial-relations department of the California Institute of Technology. During the discussion of career development, we asked one of the professors how we could identify which young officers coming on the force would have the potential for becoming good managers. The professor referred to some studies that he had performed and explained to us that, in his opinion, we should examine the attributes of the mothers of the officers under consideration. He said this was the most reliable way of determining which men would be the most responsible and goal oriented. In other words, he was saying that a mother has a more profound influence upon the development of her children than the father.

I believe this is one of the reasons women are to be kept pure. They are the essential link in the socialization process of young human beings. The type of people we have in our society fifteen years from now is related to the type of women we have as mothers today. To say that the women who rock the cradles shape the nation is a profound truth.

The nature of my job exposes me to a lot of seedy characters and perverted life-styles. Although I think it's important to share much of my professional life with Esther, there are some aspects of the job which I will not share. Some of the language, details of torture murders, or sickening specifics of a child-molestation case are better left unsaid.

Another way of protecting her is with chivalry. This, too, is a biblical principle. "You husbands likewise, live with your wives in an understanding way, as with a weaker vessel, since she is a woman; and grant her honor as a fellow-heir of the grace of life . . ." (1 Peter 3:7 NAS).

Being courteous to our wives is a way of saying, "I love you." Opening the car door, throwing your coat over her in a rainstorm, holding her arm while you're walking, just the small, gentle ways of granting her the honor she deserves as a woman: We are instructed to show this kind of attentiveness.

The Physical and Mental Nourishment of Your Wife

Men are instructed to "nourish and cherish" their wives (see Ephesians 5:29 NAS). Nourishment includes all of the dimensions of living: physical, mental, and spiritual. Physical nourishment means more than providing food on the table. It means that we should be interested in the entire physical well-being of our wives. During the child-rearing years, especially, the physical pressures on a wife and mother are extremely demanding. I think a husband who really loves his wife will relieve her of some of the household chores and help with the children. He should help ease some of the excess physical demands upon her body.

Also, I believe we should encourage our wives to keep in shape by playing tennis or golf, or bicycling. About four years ago I noticed that Esther was complaining of fatigue. I bought her a running outfit and shoes and began to jog with her. Today she feels much better—and looks spectacular!

A husband should be concerned about the mental or emotional well-being of his wife. Being a successful person is having a good self-image. A good husband works hard at developing the personal worth of his wife. This is opposite of identifying weaknesses and focusing attention upon them. It doesn't mean you assume an ostrich stance toward shortcomings, but center on the positive characteristics of your wife.

A couple of Esther's strengths lie in her creativity and musical ability. Although she has one of the best voices I've heard, initially she wasn't very confident about her talent. However, over a period of years, I encouraged her to use her singing ability. I found it was important to purchase some sound equipment and tape background music to assist her in developing her voice. Today she has a real ministry in music.

Another practical way of nourishing your wife is to allow her the opportunity for diversionary experiences. She needs to get out of the house and have a change of scene. Several years ago Esther joined with three other women to form a singing quartet. This meant rehearsing one night a week and occasionally going out to give programs. My first reaction was to discourage her. I didn't like sitting home alone at night or baby-sitting the kids, but I'm glad now that I resisted that selfish urge. It was healthy for her and opened up doors of musical opportunity.

Whatever your wife's interests, you should encourage her to develop them. This is the biblical way of expressing love.

Spiritual Nourishment

Although much of this is covered in the chapter, "Delegated by God," there are some practical ways to promote the spiritual health of your wife. For instance, after church we discuss the pastor's message, sharing how God has spoken to us through the teaching. Reading the Scriptures every night before we retire is another way of spiritual nourishment. There are very few nights in twenty-five years that we haven't done this. After reading a chapter, we briefly comment on some of the principles. We have built this habit pattern, and it doesn't seem right to retire without doing this. Afterwards, we have prayer together.

When I leave Esther in the morning, I pray for her in the car while I'm driving the freeway to work. This is probably the best spiritual food I can supply her with, and it doesn't make the traffic seem so bad, either.

Love Your Best Friend

Your wife should be your best friend. First Corinthians 13:7 (NAS) says that love "bears all things, believes all things, hopes all things, endures all things." You should expect the very best of your wife and defend her at all times. Being loyal to her is a way of expressing love.

I'm sure you've been out with a couple who spend much of the time tearing each other down in front of you. The wife may belittle her husband; the husband may openly criticize his wife. True love defends the wife, even outside of her presence.

True Love Is Forgiving

Love "does not act unbecomingly; it does not seek its own, is not provoked, does not take into account a wrong suffered" (1 Corinthians 13:5 NAS). True love doesn't keep track of faults or keep books on wrongdoings for future reference.

I remember responding to a family feud a few years ago, in which a woman had stabbed her husband. He was seriously injured, but he survived. As we conducted the investigation, the wife told us that the reason she assaulted her husband was because of something which had occurred five years prior. She had never forgotten it.

The natural thing to do is remember, when a confrontation occurs, to bring back all of the old, dirty laundry. He wants to settle the account with her; she gripes over the faults he may have.

The Bible says you shouldn't keep track of past wrongs.

Honeymoon Continued

If you want to have a beautiful wife, never stop courting her. Remember those little things you did before you were married? Those little demonstrations of love should never stop. Some good friends of ours gave us their cabin at Lake Arrowhead to use for two weeks of our honeymoon. As we were being given instructions about the cabin, where the key was, how to turn on the water, and all of those details, our friends gave us some lasting advice. They said, "Never stop working on your relationship; don't ever take each other for granted."

Basically, women are romantic. Your wife loves the little things: a flower brought to her when you come home, a special treat from the market, an unexpected phone call, little presents at unexpected times. She'll love it.

When Esther and I jog, I complete the course before she does. Along the route there are some eucalyptus trees, which have aromatic leaves. I like to pull some of those leaves and smell them while I run. I have a particular corner, which I've told Esther about, where I drop my handful of leaves. Esther looks for them as she runs by, because they are a message from me. It simply says, "I love you."

Are you a good husband? Take a look at your wife. Are you nourishing her physically, mentally, and spiritually? Are you protecting her; are you loyal to her? Are you really her best friend? Are you forgiving? Are you still courting her as a lover?

We have the instruction manual, men; the directions are there for us to use. Having a beautiful wife is one of the greatest goals for every married man. I know: I have one.